The Intimacy of Strangers

The Intimacy of Strangers

North Shore Poetry Project

Edited by
Philip Porter and Andy Kissane

PRET A PORTER PUBLISHING

© This collection Philip Porter and Andy Kissane 2018

This book is copyright. Apart from any fair dealing for the purposes of study and research, review or as otherwise permitted under the Copyright Act, no part may be produced by any process without written permission. Poets retain copyright of their poems and inquiries should be directed to the poet concerned.

First published in 2018 by Pret a Porter Publishing
13 Oakville Road
Willoughby NSW 2068
www.northshorepoetryproject.com

National Library of Australia
Cataloguing in Publication Entry:
Porter, Philip; Kissane, Andy
The Intimacy of Strangers
ISBN: 9780648410706
1.Title.
A821.3

The title of this anthology, The *Intimacy of Strangers* is taken from Philip Porter's poem 'urban affection'.

Cover Image:
Grace Cossington Smith (Australia, b.1892, d.1984)
The Lacquer Room 1936
oil on paperboard on plywood, 74.0 x 90.8 cm
Art Gallery of New South Wales
Purchased 1967
© Estate of Grace Cossington Smith
Photo: AGNSW, Jenni Carter
Used with permission.

Typeset and designed by Christine Bruderlin
Cover design by Christine Bruderlin
Printed by Lightning Source International
Published by Pret a Porter Publishing

Dedicated to John Upton,

Poet and Playwright, 1939–2017

Contents

Introduction

This Anthology, *The Intimacy of Strangers*, is the second anthology of the North Shore Poetry Project (NSPP) which stumbled into existence in May, 2012 amid the cramped benches and trestle tables of Kalay's Kitchen, then onto Rubino's Italian eatery, also in Willoughby. We went from the best falafel between here and Beirut to the best risotto between here and Milano. We have now taken up residence at The Incinerator, another excellent Willoughby restaurant, which has the best everything between here and anywhere. *A Patch of Sun* covered the dinners from our first Poetry Night in 2012 to the last one in 2014. *The Intimacy of Strangers* goes from March 2015 to March 2018.

We have more local poets, about twenty-five, but the philosophy of the NSPP has not changed. Our aim is to bring the best Australian poets to the district and to provide a venue for emerging and local poets to perform their work. We have become a genuine and viable community of poets.

Poetry has become the soft tissue of connection between people who would otherwise have never met, never exchanged the deepest of feelings and thoughts, never have become good friends. It is ironic, given the accolades social media attracts, that poetry is the best short cut to getting to know other people. It doesn't take many poems about loss, love, aloneness, God and no God for a poet's heart and mind to be exposed and responded to. It brings intimacy where there was inordinate privacy, community where there was just a passing of strangers.

Poetry and its sharing gives 'place' to those of us who have none and understanding of 'place' to those who can identify with such a notion. It creates a space between the earnest and the imaginary the entering of which, as Seamus Heaney offers, fills us 'with a momentary sense of freedom and wholeness,' allowing us to 'transform the familiar into something rich and strange.'

This anthology follows the chronological order of the poetry nights over the last three years, with the menu for each night starting the relevant chapter, as well as a short teaser of each poet's work. Each night, or chapter, includes the work of featured and local poets, and although we don't know for sure, we estimate that at least half of the poems in this book were actually read on one of these nights. This book is, in part, a physical record of a number of dynamic and memorable evenings of live poetry.

The poetry dinners have a reach that extends beyond Sydney's north shore as $5 per dinner is donated to WestWords, which supports young writers in the Western Suburbs of Sydney with master classes, numerous school based writing programs, as well as staging literary festivals in the region.

This anthology has been dedicated to the writer, John Upton, whose work opens our collection. John was a professional dramatist for twenty-seven years and an accomplished writer of both drama and comedy. John wrote extensively for television, stage and film. He won an AWGIE for Best New Play in 1985 for his play *Machiavelli, Machiavelli* and wrote for more than twenty Australian TV shows. His poetry collection, *Embracing the Razor*, was published by Puncher & Wattmann in 2014. We were privileged to have John read for us in March 2015.

So here we have it, in *The Intimacy of Strangers*, a meeting of established and local poets in a café in Australian suburbia reading to locals who are hungry for poetry and intimacy, for pleasures that engage the mind and the heart, at least for one night.

—Andy Kissane and Philip Porter

John Upton & Tricia Dearborn

Menu

Bread and piadina served with extra virgin olive oil
and balsamic vinegar
Marinated olives
Sliced prosciutto di Parma
Grilled zucchini with herbs
Semi-roasted tomatoes with garlic crumbs
Bruschetta with sautéed mixed mushrooms and parmesan

❧

Risotto with pumpkin and sage

❧

Rocket, pear, and fennel salad with parmesan
Roasted potatoes
Broccolini with almonds and lemon

❧

Grilled John Dory fillet with a lemon butter sauce

❧

My mother used to kiss the clothes to find
if they were dry; years later, I still do it.
Among the sheets and towels, you search for things.
—John Upton from 'Sheet Music'

vague forms   phantasms   float past us
coming into being and going
inventive shapes   unformed   forming
bearing their own light   fluorescent
—Rosemary Huisman from 'it is as if'

Romance began when she left the class,
their fingers touched as if by chance
and smiles took on more meaning,
—Col Grant from 'Braided'

Besieged by infant need,
surprised by sorrow, laughter, eros,

we brim, we drip.
—Tricia Dearborn from '[1] Hydrogen'

Sheet Music

My mother used to kiss the clothes to find
if they were dry on winter afternoons
(us at the clothesline, me just eight or nine),
her lips more sensitive than fingers, sifting
the feel of damp from cold. She'd strip the sheets,
arms regular as scything, hand them, rumpled,
for me to bend down to the basket. Matching
each other's moves, we never had to speak.

Then back together to the living room,
cane basket handles in my hands. Inside,
an automatic dance, uncomplicated,
habitual—a bunched up, twisted sheet,
she'd smile and take one end and I the other,
we'd fold it first in half, then stretch it flat
and pull diagonally, left and right.
So routine, this. Our practised eyes would catch
and comfortably pass. Our fingers had
the right small pressure, never tugging corners
loose. We'd fold lengthways again, and stretch.
I'd raise my arms above my head, she'd step
towards me and the downward loop would always
miss the floor. She'd take my corners, brushing fingers
and I'd let go precisely. Now she'd tuck
the folded ends between her chest and chin,
adjust her hands, then let the fabric fall,
folding itself in half. Enough was all.

My mother used to kiss the clothes to find
if they were dry; years later, I still do it.
Among the sheets and towels, you search for things.

Angel

My father used to call my mother 'angel'
during the war, before the war between
them first broke out, before the fusillades,
the rain, the sodden jungle and the sudden
sunshine, the laughter, rage, the fists, the sullen
getting-on-with-it, before all that,
he wrote to her as 'angel' from his own war,
from the steamy, deadly jungle where he fought
thousands of airlift miles removed from her,
almost as far as later, often, when
they were very close. She kept his letters
in a metal box under their double bed,
she tied them up in bundles with pink ribbon,
perhaps by date, I never looked, being seven,
and embarrassed by this written nakedness
I found when she was shopping. I remember
seeing 'angel' rendered in his hand
and retreating under fire, too aware of
the hand-to-hand, the hand to face, her long-fused
burning rage at finding that her life,
being captured, was confined in this internment camp
of barbed wire and beer, his dull lack of ambition,
his rage against her rage, and children, children,
unbidden in faith and Catholic comfort, each
a map of love and duty, but a mouth to feed.
Having made that double bed, they lay in it,
and 'angel', having been written, never quite
flew away, hiding inside that tin box,
a hostage to their war, beneath that bed,
read by a boy who couldn't understand.

Survivor

You're sitting in a mirror
in a wardrobe door
on the end of a double bed
mirror and bed both empty.
Full.
You wish this mood would shift.
The space behind the mirror is full
of clothes, all carefully hung,
blouses and skirts, all empty.

The bed in the mirror
is full of conversation,
some of it lewd, some of it loud,
some of it angry.
The mirror is a pond
full of flung stones.
You walk into the hall
the pond empties
while still remaining full and fit
for drowning in.

Hidden

Stretching up to look for a salad bowl,
I've found that you're a stranger,
Fifty-one red boxes of what killed you
bring you back instantly
months later. Why hide them?
I've no idea,
the blind geography
of long-term lovers. All I have left of you
is love and questions. And,
rage. I
take them down, tile after cardboard tile.
All empty. Why not throw them out? Why
stash all this empty air
for me to tumble in? And yet, another
part of me is grateful.
They give you back—
a secret you
I knew I knew but didn't. That private you
who couldn't make decisions.
Calm,
I catch the red-stained packets in a bin,
I click the door-lock, step onto the terrace.
I flick your lighter
I burn these inoffensive, murderous
cartons, I burn them one by one, I burn them
like cigarettes,
chain-smoking emptiness.

Crossing Galata, Istanbul

Flying fish
on Galata Bridge,
rods bowing and bobbing
like supplicants at a vizier's audience.
Each fisher has his own bait bucket
and elbow room.
I'm for the fish, somehow. Down there
there's piscine stitching of continents, Europe and Asia.
It's important work matched by the pumping ferries.
Passing between
the poles of then and now
I cross their sunshine,
a fish caught
in a rip of time, the zip of bait, the howl
of hook in mouth—it flips me
onto this bridge and off, too scrappy a catch,
victim of cheap jet fuel and wanderlust
saved for another day.

A visit from the dead

A visit from the dead should be profound,
never domestic. But my wife was practical.
Last night she half-filled the electric jug,
turned it on,
set out our usual two mugs for tea.
She was wearing her blue nightdress with the pink bows
across the bodice. I said to her,
'You're dead.' She simply poured the tea, 'I'm not.'
I was definite. 'You are.' We calmly disagreed
as we did sometimes over, say, who hadn't
put milk back in the fridge, or hadn't made
a phone call. Then she said, 'How are you?'
I said, 'You're not aware?' 'Yes, I'm aware.'
We let it go, as married couples do.
I said, 'tea's nice. But I've moved onto teabags.'
She said, 'you don't play music any more.'
'Music is dangerous.' 'That's sad.' 'It is.'
'I've discovered Dante loves orchestral.'
'Which composers? Those post-Dante? Beethoven?'
'I'm not allowed to tell you.' We drank tea,
discussed Dante and Beatrice a little,
but what she said escapes me. I can't say
how or when she left again, but when I woke
knowing it wasn't true, I knew it was.

V Manifesto

Typing quickly
(comments on 1930s homelife)
I mean to tap 'trapped by poverty'
but instead hit
'trapped by poetry'—
other than a little rearrangement, r to a t,
it's the 'v' that keeps them apart

V
let free:
inverted it might keep out the rain
pushed from the vertical, enclose a fine estate—
vineyards of purple grapes
peopled with poets

V
for a Henry might denote a king
for a clock-watcher, time to clear the desk
for an opera, an Act to sing and die
gloriously, in 'full-throated ease'
taken into heaven

V
allowed to lead, pipes a fine dance:
veracity
vivacity
vitality—
the very truth of life

V
Vote
Write on the placards:
> Make poetry not poverty!
Circle the House, chanting:
> Politics for poetry not poverty!

Viva! Viva!

it is as if

in dreams   we return to the sea
down to the shore   devolving
at the shore's edge   moving
into the warm white flow and ebb   receding
the sun strikes light   translucent
the surface   the green flow of the surface
rushes to cooler water   takes us
out beyond the breakers   pulls us
down   deeper and darker
and deeper   blue   indigo
ink to darkness

in which

vague forms   phantasms   float past us
coming into being and going
inventive shapes   unformed   forming
bearing their own light   fluorescent
suddenly illuming   vanishing to ultra-violet
indifferently tried   discarded
nurtured or miscarried
rocked in the lap slap of the ocean's tides
grouping and falling apart
intelligible becoming
unintelligible being

in which

we are/are not   the old temptation
how easier it is to stay here
amino acids   mindless
letting the spacetime worlds spin as they will
forgoing the doing of hands   the seeing of eyes
the delving and spinning   the planting and building up
families - tribes - towns - nations   and the tearing down
feud and battle and war   this evolution
exacting its price again   and again
the dream-tide   carries us
flotsam and jetsam   casts us

into the waking day

en passant

a cheese plate
or more accurately, a cheese tray
round, plastic, two-handled
decorated—photo-realistically, iconically—
with brie? comté? roquefort?
an extravagance of cheeses
straining a tourist vocabulary
wedges cut, waiting to be
recognised, ordered
presented on the tray
eaten

all this in a newsagent's window in an unremembered village
stopped in for the usual reasons, the stretching of legs

We stroll around.

a church
or more accurately, a basilica
a small basilica as befits a small village
but semi-circular, in the Italian style, the interior
nave? apse? transept?
imagined, small Roman bricks
red-darkened, pre-mediaeval
eluding a tourist history
weeds encircling the walls
the building locked
silent

back at the newsagent's, where we buy the cheese tray
and enquire: *la basilique*? Yes, Roman, possibly to be demolished soon

We drive on.

Aylan Kurdi

Did you hear the sand's slow dropping
in the egg timer for soft-boiled eggs?

Did you hear the sand's slow slopping
in the shallows under skinny little legs?

Did you hear the sand's heavy sound
on the simple wooden coffin in the ground?

So cry our sorrow for a new-drowned boy
who'll never know tomorrow!

Roosting

The sun has declined
late in the day
as it usually does
to the west
with the ocean's
moon-fed urgent pulses
as the wavelets slap
the sand and leave it
wavelet-dented too.

Wattlebirds argue
for roosts,
just as homeless men
do on covered
railway stations.

An Affair

In central Chatswood
by the railway station
nestles a cloud factory
making white cumuli
that drift due south
in midsummer,
past painted ladies
from East Cammeray
humming their swains
sweet beguiling refrains
while waiting for a chance
to score romance
or even more,
at home or
far away.

Downdraft

The chopper was poised
on a column of noise
drumming down
on Chatswood
with its searchlight
baring nothing
more exciting
than a daily
traffic jam
of those
commuting
to home again,
willing wage slaves,
not a terrorist in sight.

Braided

Romance began when she left the class,
their fingers touched as if by chance
and smiles took on more meaning,
became directed as they strolled,
still separate to their cars.

Romance followed its normal course,
meeting, parting, delight and insecurity,
By physics alone her uncle had tried
to find the half-life of love
but the course of love
followed the banks
of a braided river.

Feminines

A distaff quintet in Rose Cottage
to drown my uncles' decibels
with two school teachers
imparting basic skills,
arithmetic of course
& inflected English.

The rest an unusual group
preceded by the tutors
all quietly recondite;
dress shop owner,
psychiatric nurse
and, farmed out
across the Severn Vale,
a butcher becoming richer
from her sanguine business.

Too many to fit the Cottage
with its ack ack gun crew.

The changes

Kissing Louise was a bell. Unlike
the chimes of the genteel drawing-room clock
it gave no warning before it struck.

It was more like the shock of the extra-early
morning alarm
on the day of the journey.

Or the sudden shrilling of a schoolroom bell,
calling me in
to a strange new lesson.

It rang sweet as a tardy dinner gong
summoning me to a meal
of scent and heat.

Resonated like a great church bell
calling the villagers over fields
to christenings, to benedictions.

My throat sang my body
swung my skin shone
and my old life shivered and fell from me

and lay like the sweat of the ringers in the tower.

Come in, lie down

I'm new to you and your let's-get-to-it.
Flat on my back that first time
not five minutes after the front door

snicked behind you. New to this
excoriating tenderness, passion
that leaves me stubble-scraped and scabbed.

The shock of those minuscule nipples!
The lean hairy thigh that met my palm
and made me laugh out loud. Later you asked

was it OK, for sex with an alien?
Women are sea-creatures, you said,
one hand curved at the soft swell of my thigh.

Like seals. And men are goats. I like you
inside me, when I want it. I like how you held my hair back
that first time we stood there kissing. You come

so close to sating me with touch, stroke into me
relaxation I rarely know;
round up and banish ancient threats

whose names I'm beginning not to recognise. Still—
I miss that brine-lapped cleft, the way that sealskin
glides on sealskin. One day I must

go down to the seas again.

[1] Hydrogen

From *Autobiochemistry*

Most of earth's hydrogen is not free
in the atmosphere, diatomic,

but tethered to oxygen, in water—
the human body's solvent.

Conceived in oozing warmth
we grow in a sealed-off sea.

Once born,
we require regular watering;

in the name of homoeostasis
our bodies regularly wring us out.

Besieged by infant need,
surprised by sorrow, laughter, eros,

we brim, we drip.

[20] Calcium

From *Autobiochemistry*

A flask is laid on the electronic scale
and tared to zero. I start with a small job lot,
topped up with smaller and smaller

increments. Index finger gently taps
the silver spatula's side, loosing a miniature
sheet of fine unseasonable snow.

In nature this white powder begins
as millions of tiny skeletons, compressed
by their own multitudinous weight

and the roaring bulk of the sea. Now it will buffer
the pH of the medium, allow me to cultivate
many crinkled circular sheets of mould.

I don't know why I'm growing mould.
I don't know what I will do with my life.
But watching and measuring I accrete

habits of precision, observation; learn
the power of purposeful repetition, the thrill
when the first portion added is exact.

Perimenopause as rocket science

From *The change: some notes from the field*

you know
the instant of ignition
because it feels like you're standing

directly under those roaring jets
no way out now
you're strapped in

pointed towards
the blue
that will become a coruscating dark

let's hope you can handle
some solid g's
as you take off

another layer, sweating
on your trajectory
to an undiscovered world

Memo

lunch break. pigeons scatter
before me, one swooping up

to pose regally
on top of the war memorial

I lie face down, forehead resting
on the backs of my hands

inhale the smell of buffalo grass
and earth, turn my head

sideways and consider
this version of a bird's eye view

back at my desk I see patterns,
hieroglyphics, a strange language

impressed on the skin
of my inner arms

I'm sure I can read it
I'm sure it says: give up your day job

Andy Kissane & Eileen Chong

Menu

Bread / Piadina with extra virgin olive oil and balsamic vinegar
Marinated olives
Sliced prosciutto di Parma
Grilled eggplant
Roasted pumpkin and sage
Bruschetta with white bean, rosemary and smoked paprika

❧

Risotto with celeriac and leeks

❧

Fennel, apple and celery salad
Roasted potatoes and parsnips with thyme
Sautéed Italian rapini with garlic and chilli

❧

Roast beef sirloin with mustard

❧

I couldn't help myself. I said, 2000 years and all
it amounts to is traffic flow. And you gave me
that look and I knew: *Eli, Eli*, it is finished.
—Andy Kissane from '3am'

> I thought of Time, the constant thief, relentless and without relief;
> devouring all before and after with sly aware and sullen laughter,
> meting out with stony gaze a genesis and end of days;
> of lives, their coming and their going, the tides of life, the to, the froing;
> —Charles Murray from 'Gravitational Wave'

Everything glows golden,
Sunset's laudation to the bay.
Dancing through the archways of every bar and café.
The paint is peeling, and the window glass is falling out
Rum the only thing in danger, of never running out
—Sarnie Hay from 'Sunset over Havana'

> At fourteen, there are days when you
> don't speak beyond one syllable.
> Here, we're not allowed to talk
> and for once, it simply doesn't matter.
> —Alison Gorman from 'Heart Meditation'

Like the rose, so many shades of blood and white.
One birthday I woke to find peonies the shade
of night's red stabbed in a vase. Their hearts:
so closed, so full of mystery.
—Eileen Chong from 'Only a Peony'

Loaves and Days

He throws the ball of dough
up above his head. His eyelids
are thick with broken sleep,
his hands white with flour. Lightning
hands. There is a rhythm in this tossing
and catching that is mesmerising,
the unconsciousness of hands
that fling and pluck and fling again.
As if the precious organs of the body
have replaced the dough—a liver
striving for the ceiling, a kidney falling
to an open palm. A heart that is stretched,
kneaded and pumped, then plonked
on the waiting tray. Loaves edging forward
on rollers into a heat that will turn
sourdough golden and cook the crust
of the pumpernickel until it's as hard
as a fist. Loaves running together
like the hours and minutes spent
in the fluorescent glare of Gino's Bakery.
When he watches the last of them
slide away, he only sees bread,
not the tables they'll adorn like cut flowers,
not the man who never cuts an even slice,
or the woman who lifts up the rye
on a breadboard shaped like a bell.
He's had enough of this job, doesn't care
if he never bakes another loaf,
but he loves this moment
when he steps out of the furnace
into the cool darkness of a Petersham street,
runs his hand through his hair
and gazes up at the black wires
where the dawn birds line up,
fidgeting like choirboys about to sing.

The Street Vendor's Lament

I am five years old; I earn my own pay.
I carry, wash and cook from morning to night.
I call out 'Enchilada, Enchilada' for ten coins a day.

I roll out tortillas, flat and white as clay,
warm them on a griddle, flip them when they're right—
I am seven years old and I earn my own pay.

Other children stare at me: I can smell their dismay.
Because I don't go to school, can't read or write,
I sing 'Enchilada, Enchilada' for ten coins a day.

I dream of another life, the games I could play.
I'd love to kick a football or run with a kite,
for I am nine years old and I earn my own pay.

The money helps my family, it keeps hunger at bay.
But I can't help thinking: Is this my birthright?
To chant 'Enchilada, Enchilada' for ten coins a day?

I long to start afresh, I want to run away,
leave this street, the black stove, the harsh city light.
I am eleven years old yet I earn my own pay;
I cry out 'Enchilada, Enchilada' for ten coins a day.

The Carpet Weaver

Kashan, Iran

Every day Azra walked to her uncle's workshop
to weave rugs too precious to walk on. Carpets
destined for America or Paris, where they might

adorn polished floorboards or be proudly hung
on the wall of a billiard room. At seven Azra
learnt how to beat down the threads with a heavy

iron comb. At nine she graduated to the loom,
her long, nimble fingers tying the Senneh knot
as tight and as tiny as her uncle required.

You can learn the history of a tribe from rugs,
her uncle liked to say—their wars, their religion
and culture, even their decadence. All day

Azra bent over the loom, carrying a jumble
of colours and knots in her head. A prince
with a falcon clinging to his wrist, a tiger

stalking the spotted ibex. All day she laboured
in a windowless room that was hot, stuffy.
Sometimes the children's voices mingled

and pealed like goats' bells, sometimes
there was only the sound of their breathing,
the pliant silk, the wind made by the speed

of their fingers. Occasionally, a girl would brag
of her accomplishment and they'd count knots,
or race to tie off the last thread in the green eye

of a dragon. At eighteen the doctor tells Azra
that her pelvis is so small, so misshapen that it will
surely crush a baby's skull. When the time comes,

she must have a caesarian section. If only I could
get that far, she thinks, as she takes the bloodied
pad out of her underwear. Her weaving has led

to this, just as the path leads to the hammam,
the bazaar, the Mosque. Tonight Azra will cry
as she tells her husband that their boy—she

doesn't know why but she thinks of the baby
as a boy—is lost, like the last one. There will be
no turquoise gems, no new rug, no days

of sunlight and birdsong, no table laden
with food and refreshments. There will be
no need to count the weeks, no cause to stack

the swaddling cloths in a corner of their home.
There's no point trying again, she thinks, I am
as helpless as a silkworm boiled in its own cocoon.

3am

Along High Street, the window in the white Cortina
right down, the air rushing in, my foot on the accelerator
beating time to the electric fizz of Johnny B. Goode,

all evening my hand inside your jumper—what bliss!
Street lights flashing past like beacons of joy.
Everything went so well until you found Jesus.

It never works after that. When you said,
if you ask Jesus into your life you'll never miss
another green light, or wait for a parking space,

I couldn't help myself. I said, 2000 years and all
it amounts to is traffic flow. And you gave me
that look and I knew: *Eli, Eli*, it is finished.

The Book of Screams

Each day in hospital I wake
to a reading from *The Book of Screams.*
It comes, apparently, from the bathroom
situated two-thirds of the way along the hall.
No one talks while the screams linger.
I pass the time by counting in my head.
Thirty-five. Seventy-two. One hundred
and nine. Two hundred and thirty-one.
The screams are high-pitched and continuous,
as if she has been chosen for her ability
to hold the note, to produce abrasive chords
when her lungs must be almost airless and empty.
The ruckus shakes the thin partition around my bed,
it rattles the cups and saucers in the kitchen,
and threatens to shatter the high frosted panes
of glass that leach feeble light onto the floorboards.

At midday and again in the evening I reluctantly
listen to recitals from *The Book of Screams.*
Afterwards, the ward is sombre with silence.
By the third day, I cannot bear it any longer,
I tear the bandage from my eyes and march
down the corridor to see for myself, drawn
to the noise the way iron filings are attracted
to magnetic north. Two nurses cradle
a young girl, supine, in a bathtub.
Her eyes are closed, her lips collapse
into an involuntary O that corresponds
to the coordinates of her mouth. Her skin,
though I am not sure you can still call
it that, is the black of newly laid bitumen.

Impossible to comprehend agony—
to understand how one scream seems

to necessitate another, to grasp how a voice
can travel over rice paddies and rubber plantations,
under jungle canopies and down boulevards
resplendent with French architecture, before lifting
into the flying arches and buttresses of the mind,
until we are all dwelling in a cathedral of screams
whose substantial form cries out for mercy.

But I have no mercy to give. I gaze
in dumb horror at her right leg, where
the white ghost of her femur shines
through murky water, at the charred
oozing mess of a knee. Her body is
no more than a diaphanous veil hanging
between this world and the next.

Later, they tell me about the morning
of the bombing and its aftermath.
Now, when I hear the word *napalm,*
I remember that girl's face,
her eyes opening as I turn
to leave, her raw cries staying
with me and spiralling outwards,
forever travelling, like radio waves
rolling end over end
into the windless chasms of space.

It Begins with Darkness

People file into the room, find their seats,
fill up the air with chatter. The stage
is bare except for a leather couch
and a lamp on a chrome and bakelite stand.
It's meant to be an old factory converted
to an apartment—exposed pipes, a ceiling
fit for a cathedral, polished oak floorboards.
A man dressed in black makes an announcement
about mobile phones. The lights go down.
I don't know what I'm doing here,
I just know that this is theatre, my son an actor.

I hear his voice before I see him. It's as loud
as the wind swatting at a loose sheet of corrugated iron
on the chook shed. When he comes on stage
he swears five times in the first minute,
all in the presence of a lady. I've a good mind
to go down and slap him about the face,
except that I'm sitting right in the middle of the row
and it wouldn't be easy getting past all those knees.
Then I remember that he's pretending
to be someone else, that this is his job now.
Soon everyone is laughing—they're smiling
and nodding and taking in every move my son makes.

I've never been to a play before. It's not
boilermaking, not the flying sparks from an arc welder,
not the precision required for a submarine hull,
nor the relief of taking off your helmet,
gloves and apron and enjoying the coolness
of a harbour breeze as you eat your lunch,
but it is, I guess, a different kind of trade.
I watch more and it all happens before my eyes
and I can see that he loves this lady,

everyone can see it and I want to say, 'Son,
what are you afraid of?' I want to reach out
and lift him up as I did when he was two
years old, riding a supermarket trolley
and screaming as if he'd just discovered
the power of his lungs. But I can't touch him now
or even talk to him and I have this feeling
that it will turn out badly, like the week you have
the numbers in Lotto, but forget to buy the ticket.

The stage is dark again and he's not swearing now
and the lady's really pleased to see him
and she burns this scrap of paper and it flares up,
bright and yellow in the darkness
and the flame flickers across his forehead
and I glimpse in my son's face the unmistakable
features of my father who is ten years dead.
Although the three of us won't ever meet again,
I'm sure Dad would have loved this—a story
that takes a whole evening in the telling
and a small fire that leaps and glows
and transfixes us, for as long as it burns.

Gravitational Wave

We heard in wonderment the tale, a new infinity of scale,
of time, a gravitational wave, a billion light year sonic rave
as two black holes in pas de deux, stygian dervishes whirling through
the deepest space, man never knew of time, a metronomic wave,
the ebb and flow, the undulave; washing over thought profound,
new knowledge beyond light and sound; with senses reeling in sensation,
dynamic, thrilled imagination;
And . . .
I thought of Time, the constant thief, relentless and without relief;
devouring all before and after with sly aware and sullen laughter,
meting out with stony gaze a genesis and end of days;
of lives, their coming and their going, the tides of life, the to, the froing;
the deeper thought, the never knowing, the sower and the seeds for
        sowing,
the secrets all their silence keeping, nightmares feeding on our sleeping,
the Reaper and his silent reaping;
But . . .
I mark my life from time AD, blest thrice by God's own Trinity
of Father, Son and Holy Ghost, the Son of whom I love the most,
whose humanness is just like me, whose power transcends that gravity;
whose saving Grace is there for all, through the billion light year faint
        footfall
upon this world, our living place, our common Earth,
our global home in Space.

At My Father's Knee

At my father's knee I listened to the music of his soul;
From the classics he, enraptured, would lullaby a barcarolle,
And with my eyes closed to his dreaming, sought the solace of his bliss,
As my bones soaked up the old songs of which I reminisce.
He conducted symphonies and preludes as if they were his own
And when he held me to his heart we were a perfect metronome.
He'd whisper, 'listen now', his earnestness would hold me in the thrall
Of nocturne, waltz and overture, or sonorous massed chorale;
'That's "Nabucco", son, a wondrous piece,' and as the voices' weep washed
        o'er us,
I felt my soul transported there to join the Hebrew slaves in chorus.
Oh, this was more than ecstasy, it was music to the brim;
For the myriad shades of rhapsody were the heart and soul of him;
And the ritual of those weekend eves when the wireless set was king,
Presented concerts in our kitchen, hallmarked my life and made it sing.
I'm Dad's age now, he's long-time gone though his precious gift remains,
And in my memories' ebb and flow I hear another Chorus strains;
'It's The Nuns,' I hear him whisper, 'Anni Frind will sing and pray.'
And I've heard him all my life since, in my memories, day by day.

These Also Her Children

I wonder, now, did she name them,
I know she grieved and mourned
for sixty years and more.
She remembered always
their leaving and their going times
and would be sad for a while,
but mostly she was joyous,
smiling that soft gentle smile
only a mother's memory makes.
She knew I saw those times,
in my later years confiding
because she believed
I'd seen enough of life to understand.
In the August we had celebrated
her one hundred years of life
and after the Christmastime
before I left to travel home,
half a world away,
she held my hands,
looked beyond my presence, saying,
'Remember them on the memorial
when I go' . . . just one of a litany
of her requests, and so it was . . .
On Valentine's Day 2002,
we laid her to rest at Esker,
and by the next summer's end,
as she had asked;
Their space, their Memorare,
graven on the grey granite face,
Sarah's five miscarried babies
whom she had never forgotten.

The June Effect . . . When Winter Roared In

My courtyard Virginia stripped bare of her crimson
bedraggled and beat by the rain,
said farewell to the Autumn and all of her passion
lay bare on the lawns once again.
For Winter roared in like a wilful, wild creature,
ripped russet and gold from the vine
and the wind and the rain, without fear, without favour
was ruthless in stripping its line.
It spared no one and nothing its anger, its rages,
sought weakness in structure and plan;
Played havoc with builder and well-meaning sages,
made a nonsense of so-perfect man.
So, I'm left with the wreckage and an ongoing norm,
Red Alerts and the mayhem they bring;
Now resigned to the Winter, this near perfect storm
bends my thoughts to the coming of Spring.

The Fields of Grief . . . WW1

We went down to the fields of grief to mourn,
to offer in silence our pain;
For all the young men had perished and gone
and would never be seen again.
Blown as the bloom of a radiant rose
stripped by a wild wind and rain;
Nought but the air of their silent repose
In our souls will forever remain.
We've returned from the fields of grief once more,
We have supped at the well of tears
And tasted their sacrifice, bitterly sore;
Now we weep for the loss of their years.

Will, and That Question

Four hundred years elide and still we mind
his memory and all its works in kind;
The playhouse and the sonnets that were told,
vital today and relevant, though old.
For we who follow on his written words
build culture and the mores of the day,
hear witches cant, and sweet song of the birds
and in midsummer, all of love's a play.
While in the graveyard's dusk, lament is made
and in Elsinore, a solitary prince
equivocates, you know well what was said
without the benefit of cues or hints;
To be is to always be, forever,
as you are, beloved Bard, unanswered, never!

The Awakening

The bedroom is beginning to fill with light;
Into the garden of my quiet dreaming night.
Like a new bud on old wood;
It's blossoming understood.

Along worn out stones I softly tread,
My feet immersed in Chamomile's spongy bed.
Thoughts like Jacaranda petals fall like snow;
Illuminated by expectation, they seem to glow.

My fingers itch to touch.
God's seasons gentle flush.
Thyme and sympathy with sage
The skin of a tree withered with age.

I dream of the rose over bitter rue,
Flashes of Borage, my favourite eye shadow blue,
I meander with Daffodils, head down in solidarity,
And awake like a sunflower: wild in anarchy.

As the sun rises, round as a Hydrangea head,
I find myself singing all the way to the Garden Shed.
What lust this Eden's song does bid?
Why it's Eve's awakening from ankle to eyelid.

Uncork the Wine

Surrender recalcitrant cork
and let the captured grape,
draw from the darkened cellar
light and life again.
Graceful stripes gather
down the sides of the swirling glass,
and, my nose starts to morcellate
the heady, new aromas;
sweet cardamom and bitter chocolate,
once aged in French Hogsheads,
along the Du Midi Canal.
The first sip lingers,
silky-long in the mouth,
wrapped in warm, drowsy days.
A barge floating past Sunflower fields,
vineyards dripping with purple grapes,
at every twist and turn.
The gentle breeze through the plane trees
Lochs and sleepy villages
of mouth filling appellations.
Fruit bottled at that perfect moment,
and, now purified on my palate,
with the rich aftertaste of uncorked memories.

Whisky on the Rocks

The finger slides smoothly around the rim of Crystal—
causing it to vibrate.
Bubbles of ice fracture over the whisky underneath.
Ice gives way to fire.
Upon the tongue the line of an implacable love-song,
finds its voice in the crystal's residue;
thick and sticky like that hot summer night
we danced—heart on heart,
across the floor of the Milky Way
to the border between stillness and
movement—that never reached an end.

Sunset Over Havana

Everywhere a sound, the rhythm of son;
Salting every kiss, on the Malécon
Everyone becomes a lover with a touch,
'To Have and Have not', in Hemingway's
Havana—that he loved so much.

Everything glows golden,
Sunset's laudation to the bay.
Dancing through the archways of every bar and café.
The paint is peeling, and the window glass is falling out
Rum the only thing in danger, of never running out

Light a cigar and leave resolutions behind,
Grab a Mojito and taste Cuba, a minute at a time
Buildings keep crumbling to fall at Castro's feet.
This long-elusive city; consistent, sometimes contradictory,
And, sometimes bitter sweet.

'Am I young enough to drive this pink Chevrolet,'
I whisper to the sun, promenading behind the end of day,
'Nothing here has a used-by-date,' I imagine it to say.
So I climb behind the wheel, gently close the door.
Feeling so much younger than I've ever felt before.

Sirius is dying

Almost blind and all alone in her 10th floor room,
Myra listens for sounds, but hears only doom.
As night comes down on the million dollar view;
her SOS sign pulses the last signal of social milieu.

Sirius is dying—sinking from neglect,
Tethered to the iron Coat-hanger,
by a flimsy cord of heritage respect.
Rope vines spill from totemic, concrete blocks;
down the gap between the haves and have-nots.

Empty of working-class people—by manipulation.
Empty of the 'One-Way Jesus' man;
who believed he was there through divine collaboration
Empty of antagonism, and, a paler green anxiety.
Empty to the homeless; its vacancy such bitter irony.

The Age of Innocence

Gone the age of innocence,
Impelled by nature's knife.
Spilled like ink in the diary
Of day-to-day life.
Courage cocooned—
In a robe of worn out silk.
Beauty, like desire—just spilt milk.
Less, is better than worse,
In the growing older School;
With one golden exception to the rule.
Love remains the same
Beneath the surface of all five senses;
Measured in the moments of coincidences.
As certain as the Flanders Poppy,
Will bloom each November
Lest we forget to remember;
The age of Innocence.

Heart meditation

There are many kinds of happiness.
You sit opposite me in the library
at a table for two next to the Dixson
card catalogue—your new horn rimmed

glasses match the neat, teak drawers
with their yellowed labels. I watch you
scratch words with your favourite pen—
blue, the cap lightly chewed with thought.

You'll lay it down next to the red
and black, open a laptop and press
in earbuds. Slender fingers type,
sometimes stopping to finger comb

your hair. You're listening to a counter
tenor sing *Ombra federa anch'io*.
Above us, light pours through a glass
ceiling and runs down three tiers

of blackwood shelves. A curling bronze
staircase leads to old volumes that sit
in families of red and navy, their names
printed in gold. Griffins, rosettes and urns

decorate a travertine frieze and stained glass
windows tell the Canterbury tales. A long hand
on the old clock bounces with each minute.
The air is warm, muggy with books.

At fourteen, there are days when you
don't speak beyond one syllable.
Here, we're not allowed to talk
and for once, it simply doesn't matter.

Guan Yu

There's a statue that sits
inside my parent's front door,
next to a ginger jar crowded
with canes and umbrellas.

Carved from dark rosewood
he crouches forward on a tangled
root, as though he has something
to say. I see him through narrow

glass as I prepare to knock.
Fierce warrior with phoenix
eyes—he bears a dragon blade
and his long beard flows East.

As a child, I could never tell
if he was smiling. I tried not to look.
But today I see him. Guan Yu.
Loyal hero. Saint of war.

The dog barks my arrival
and I hear my parent's halloos
as they make their long walk
down the short hallway.

As I wait, I think about
those years I didn't visit,
the years we didn't speak.
The door opens.

Does he see how far we have come?

Rembulan spa

Ubud, Bali

Soon, Sutri will paint my nails
vivid magenta, the colour of dragon
fruit, while I rest in the deep curve

of an old teak chair. She takes my left
hand and kneads it with long, smooth
fingers, pressing tendons, stretching

my palm back until I am an Apsara,
loose enough to float my celestial limb
in a bowl of sandalwood water.

She holds my right hand, studies the thumb,
tsking at torn, reddened cuticles bitten
by disquiet, misshapen over years.

I want to curl my hand away, close it
like a lotus bud. Instead, I watch her dab
pale pink cream, until the skin cools.

Sutri props my thumb with hers, steadies
it to paint. The colour bleeds bright
from the brush. Slow, careful strokes,

Her lips twitch as she removes stray magenta
with a bud. Later, I know she'll paint
someone else's nails—shades

of bougainvillea, hibiscus or perhaps
plumbago. But now, as she fans dry
these mended hands I think of my sister,

washing my hair when I was a child.
Her careful combing, my smooth hair.
I taste the sweetness of fruit.

Panthera Leo

Lower Zambezi

Tonight, the lion is here. Right here,
near our jeep. An open jeep
with no roof, windows nor doors.
In the moonlight, he patrols thickets

of yellow finger grass that border
his pride land. I slide down the back
seat to the floor and watch with one
eye. In front, my family whisper

as Patrick changes the spotlight lens
to red. In the rosy glow, the lion shakes
his mane. He raises his vast, flat forehead
from the earth to inhale the night.

Amber eyes close and his mouth pulls
apart in a curling grimace. Four scimitar
teeth catch light as the lion tastes the air.
Sommelier of sex, he lifts his black

thatched tail and grunts. Giant testes
bob like fruit. He sprays bursts
of urine and desire into the scrub
before smelling the dirt again.

For days, we have searched for him.
Along the riverbeds at dusk
where Egyptian geese rise in pairs
from the reeds and fly low over dark water,

where Goliath herons step their faith
around crocodiles, mouths half open
in the fading heat and slick hippopotamus
leave the river with bellies as pink

as newborns to graze all night.
We searched Mopane woodlands
amongst rust and golden branches
and the deepest shadows of a Winter thorn

forest but we didn't find him.
Tonight the lion is here padding
towards the jeep, towards my seat.
And just, when I feel I must call

out like a startled puku, a breeze
seduces him with a new scent.
He turns and walks away
—a shiver in the grass.

Viva La Vida

Frida Kahlo writes to Diego River, July, 5th, 1954

Soon, I will leave you Diego.
Death will unpin me from this bed
to float with Noguchi's butterflies
into our blue walled garden.
I will rest upon the pyramid
among the pots and cacti
and drink nectar from the orange
dahlia that grows between your idols.
I will watch over Casa Azul,
and you, *mi amor*.

But first, I must finish
this painting. It is the sweet, pink flesh
of watermelon. I love the way it hides
beneath it's dark, green skin.
Tell me, what shall I call it?
Los sandias? No. I want a message
for our comrades in Guatemala.
Let it come to me in my final
brushstrokes and I shall write
it here on this slice.

I want to paint in the garden today
with the spider monkeys eating fruit
from my hand. I want Bonito to perform
his best parrot tricks for a pat of butter
and Granizo to look at me with his fawn eyes.
Mother said that you and I were like a marriage
between an elephant and a dove. But you are a toad,
Diego and the greatest accident of my life.
Not even my sister was safe
in your slippery hands. *Bastardo!*
I took lovers as balm but the truth is

I love you more than my own skin.
Promise me that you will burn my body
when I have gone. Ask the women to dress
me in my white Yalalag huipil, to braid my hair
with flowers and to put on my rings.
Play music and drink tequila. Ask Chavela
to sing *Paloma Negra* to me. Set fire
to my bed and watch my body burn.
Until then, I will keep painting words
onto watermelon.

ALISON GORMAN

Ghost Ranch, 1949

After Georgia O'Keefe

Sometimes, I like to imagine
I lived then. I'd travel to Abiquiu
in the spring by train, chug my way
through mountains, dotted with spruce
and boulders until I glimpse views
of the Chama river carving a blue sweep
through tundra meadow, the aspens
and cottonwoods in new leaf.

Perhaps I was drawn by paintings
of the Pedernal, your private mountain
given to you by God, you say,
it's flinty caprock as flat as a canvas.
How do we meet? It doesn't matter.
I'd visit you in your hacienda,
a symmetry of red earth walls with a lush
garden of vegetables and jimson weed.

Would you welcome me with a salad
of lovage? Or prickle like the cactii
on your porch? I want to sit in the cool,
white of your living room and see
your mountain change from mauve
to deep red. We could drink tea
at your dining table and listen
to Gershwin or Bach.

Maybe, we'd talk about the colours
of music or small flowers, like hollyhock
and larkspur that no one really sees
until you paint them big. I wouldn't mention
Freud nor my carnal thoughts when I look
at *Black Iris*. No, I wouldn't ask about Alfred
or those broken months in Bermuda
when you couldn't paint.

Let's drive out to the White Place
in your model A Ford. We'll walk
the pink clay of badlands (littered with pallid
hoodoos and colourless spires), fossick
in the scree for bleached bones strewn
amidst tumbleweed. As you lean back
on the limestone cliff, I'll watch you
sketch a cow skull that you imagine

               is floating in the sky.

Burning Rice

I did not mean to burn the rice tonight.
'Planting rice is never fun'—generations
of men, women and children ankle-deep
in padi fields, bent double at the waist,
immersing seedlings day after day.

Finally, the harvest: sharp scythes glinting
in the afternoon sun, stalks of ripened grain tossed
into baskets strapped onto backs like babies too young
to walk. Next, the rice huller, churning husks
away from the hearts. Then the long hours polishing

each dark grain into pearly white. I'd forgotten
that brown rice needed more than double
the usual measure of water. I smelt the charring,
then saw: scorched rice like black gold,
my ancestors' ashes in a bowl.

Lu Xun, your hands

But as you look up and inhale the intoxicating smoke from your tobacco,
can you spare a thought for those scrambling to find a way
out of this nest of scorpions?
—Xu Guangping, in her first letter to Lu Xun, 1925

Lu Xun, your hands
are clasped behind your back,
across the black silk
of your scholar's dress. My eyes trace the length
of your fingers encircling your wrist. Tonight,
Lu Xun, your hands will drag
their heavy, eloquent path across
my milk-soft skin. Your mouth will cease
to form words like *liberty, ideology,*
and *compassion,* but will instead silently
enclose the peach blossoms
of my breasts.

Lu Xun, your hands are the instruments
through which you conduct
desire. In the morning, your fingers are pale
and controlled; your brush hovers
then descends upon the sheets
of rice paper. My eyes follow only
each stroke. Your thoughts
unfold before me, beginning
at the moss-green rocks. They linger
in the shade of the toothpick pavilion, beneath
its heavy jade tiles. They form a deep red,
half-moon bridge

across the rush of river
fed by the waterfall whose origin lies
in the death-grey mountains. Lu Xun,
your hands warm the wood of the pipe
that I fill. My fingers, deft as birds
in flight, strike a match-soldier. Provoked,
it flares orange and ash. Dragon,
you exhale whole curlicues of cloud. Words
as yet unformed in my mind
now go up in smoke. They too know
that I am in heaven, Lu Xun,
for your hands.

Only a Peony

There is nothing more difficult . . . than to paint a rose.
—Henri Matisse

Peony, Chinese rose, history taught me about you.
You adorned the headdresses of Manchurian princesses,
pinned above tassels that swung back and forth,
mimicking their mincing walk. An upturned bowl placed
under a platform, the sway of hands for balance. A fiction
of bound feet. Were you real, flower of fortune?

What does a peony smell like? I have nestled
my nose within their depths but breathed nothing
of their notes. Perhaps I needed to have crushed them,
smeared their juice in my hands, eaten their petals one
by one. I know that women who swallow flowers
must avoid princes, rivers and deposed emperors.

Like the rose, so many shades of blood and white.
One birthday I woke to find peonies the shade
of night's red stabbed in a vase. Their hearts:
so closed, so full of mystery. In seven days a shake
and the flowers would fall apart. I would taste
the naked heads: nothing, not even pollen, would remain.

Under the sign of *mudan*, you bought me my first gift.
Celadon-green, cool against the peach skin of my cheek.
Too big: the bangle slipped on and off my wrist. *When a man
gives you jade, it's like diamonds, only truer.* How was I to know
we were only mortal? I bound the cracks with gold.
I thought I was to die. Then it shattered into four.

In the darkness of the shophouse, arrayed on a stand:
bottles containing the essence of peonies. *Pivoine magnifica,*
the magnificent peony. Healer of the gods, I see you
tacked under the altar in a takeaway shop. On the shelf,
Guan Yu, deified, stands ready for battle. His face, painted
crimson: the shade of these peonies before rot.

We cut away the tape and unroll the carpet.
Pink and red swirls tufted in pure new wool.
Blossoms on branches form the background
to stylized cross-sections of peonies: leaves,
stems, blooms. One lady nods and smiles:
China's national flower. Is it? Am I? I've forgotten.

Magnolia

A son's birth means tragedy now.
—'Song of the War-Carts', Du Fu

I rise from my pallet: it is still dark
and the men are asleep, their naked chests
inflating and collapsing like a smith's bellows.

The moon hangs beneath the clouds: soon
autumn will arrive, winds rippling the fields.
Back in my village, the farmers are preparing

for the harvest. I press together strips of linen,
line it with moss I'd picked from the base of trees.
It is my time, and my secret. Tomorrow we advance

towards the border. The war-carts are loaded,
the horses will be tethered to their burdens.
Here the quivers of arrows wait to be spent.

I carry a skin of water and squat in the grasses.
Now it is safe to loosen my robes. Carefully, I clean myself.
Even in the dark, my hands are sticky with blood.

***

My first kill was a chicken. It was the new year.
Father handed me his knife and gestured at our hen.
She strutted around the yard, cocking her head this way

then that, scratching and searching for worms.
In the bamboo coop her brood of chicks cried warning.
I pushed up my sleeves and advanced. No fear—

we'd done this before, her and I. This was betrayal.
I carried her to the back of the hut, her heartbeat
pulsing in my palm. Her feathers so alive against my skin.

***

My faithful horse bears me for many miles, carries me
into battle, comforts me with his touch. Between my legs,
the saddle creaks my name: *Mu Lan, Mu Lan.*

Not for me the embroidered magnolias of marriage;
I give birth to nothing but blades, arrows and death.
My sword is my husband, my brothers my men.

They think me one of them. I drink sweet wine
fermented from plums; I curse and spit and plot.
I kill without mercy. Beneath my armour, secreted

in a pouch: a carved jade favour from the King.
In the night I draw my fingers across the dragon
twisting around the sun. The morning dawns emerald.

***

A soldier unfurls a banner and I plant it deep
in the soil. Another day, another frontier.
Men are busy at the fires: they grind millet

and cook it into gruel. So many mouths to feed,
so many sons, fathers, brothers . . . How much longer
before I gaze upon the lined face of my own father?

Beyond us, the mountains rise in mockery.
Wei is surrounded, corralled on all sides:
Qin, Zhao, Yan, Qi, Chu, Han . . .

If I were a hawk I would take off, wing towards
the west and the setting sun. I would hunt only
to survive, I would feather a nest, I would fly.

Painting Red Orchids

Last night, red orchids in the thatched hut burst into blossom.
Worrying about the wind and rain, unable to sleep.
—'Red Orchid', Huang Shen

My brushes hang in stillness on polished rosewood.
Weasel hair, wolf tail, mink fur. This one, an eyelash
from a leopard. The inkstone was my father's: slate

quarried from the lake where my great-grandfather
drowned himself one spring night. I scoop well-water
onto the stone and grind the inkstick back and forth.

Pine oils diffuse into the room. My wife has made
this paper with mulberry from our gardens. I lift
my brush, pull back my sleeve and saturate the hairs.

One stroke, one breath: leaves give way to blossom.
More water—rain and cloud above the trees.
Cochineal paste, jade seal—red orchids bloom on white.

Seven in the Bamboo

I'm worried I'm not political enough
—Raquel Ormella

In the morning I wake and put on my clothes
and shoes and a cap. I walk to the water's edge

past dogs, people, bicycles and boats.
The sun rises on the horizon and I sit and face

the water and think and watch the clouds and the trees.
I don't read a newspaper or buy a coffee at the café.

I go home and take a hot shower and sit with my cats.
I read a book, maybe two, write some poems perhaps.

I listen to music: the radio, sometimes, or an old song
from my collection. I stretch and lie down in the grass.

I eat something: fruit, cheese, a bowl of soup. On good days
there is chocolate. There is always a cup of tea. I don't think

about pain, or loss, or the past, although they are there.
I don't think about refugees or dead babies or chemical

warfare or Iraq or Israel. I worry I live under a rock
even as my mind winds up the wooded paths and streams

of third-century China. I imagine I am packing a frame-
and-cloth bag full of books and two changes of clothes

for a long journey into the mountains. Seven of us meet
in a bamboo grove. Two of us make love in the moonlight

after we are all drunk from pots of rice wine. Someone watches
us, but we don't care. We forget about society, about politics,

about government. We sow, we grow, we reap. We dream, we read,
we write, we paint. The notes of the zither shiver in the night air.

Kevin Hart

Menu

Bread / Piadina with extra virgin olive oil and balsamic
Marinated olives
Roasted peppers
Sautéed mixed mushrooms
Bruschetta with ricotta, semi-sundried tomato
and balsamic glaze

❧

Risotto with cauliflower, smoked mozzarella,
and toasted almonds

❧

White bean, shallot, and tomato salad with rocket
Creamy polenta
Cavalo nero

❧

Chicken cacciatore hot pot

❧

She'd left her name out in a field, she said,

But Auntie Fay had always been, well, odd,
And as those days would have at best two chords
I listened for a third with her all day.
—Kevin Hart from 'Spring Wheat'

As you speak I take a mouthful of air
as you take in mine—the exquisite
intimacy of strangers—caught stealing
chunks from each other. An urban love poem?
—Philip Porter from 'urban affection'

give me a small beacon
so that in some future
unknown space in time
I can navigate back to you
through the stars
—Frances Roberts from 'Separation'

Tears ran away and turned into poem
Rhyme spilled out of a song
Life ran away with kiss and a prayer
And soon things would go terribly wrong
—Henrietta Metcalf from 'Gypsy Road Madness'

KEVIN HART

Invective against certain months of the year

Fuck you, October, can't you even count?
You should've gone with August, months ago,
But here you are, just hanging round, like smells

Of stale fish pie forgotten in the fridge,
With all that Libra stuff, star sign for dopes,
All 'on the one hand, on the other'— shit,

It's just as bad as stupid kids dressed up as ghosts
Hands grubbing candy left out in the rain.
Is 'National Liver Month' the best you've got?

I hear you might be getting something new,
'Erectile Disability Month!' Enjoy.
I see you've brought along your buddy there,

So hey, November, dude. Flunk Math as well?
How many times you won the Nobel Prize?
You're 'National Novel Writing Month,' you say?

Well, if you wanna hang out with cheap guys
Who feel they've gotta fill up all the page,
Go right ahead! Besides, I hate the Cup:

It's always just a horse that wins the prize,
Not even Patrick White. But what gets me
Is that you're here at all, and in my way,

When sweet December's waiting next in line,
With Christmas in his smile, and my girl there,
In Melbourne, novel falling from her hand:

She's wearing dabs of perfume, nothing else,
And waiting for you guys to bugger off,
And she's the whole damn world to me, and more.

Rain

We know the rain: how April sags with clouds,
How loose rain flies for hours in baggy wind;
We know young lychee flesh of summer rain,

Mosquito rain that bites on hot, thick nights,
And ant-rain falling from fat figs up north.
We know too well dark rain that chills the heart,

Rain old as moon dust, young as moonlight; soft
Ghost rain when poor men marry, ravens too.
We live inside a prison house of rain

Then walk, at night, between small bickering lights
Along a beach: sky flashes into rain
That slaps us in the face and teases sea.

In March rain hangs in bloated cheesecloth clouds,
Unlike those blood-warm drops on August days
That splash upon our sunburned arms, unlike

May muslin rain that children try to catch.
Rain knows our faces when our children leave
In sun and rain, when friends all go to earth;

It lives upon our cheeks for days, then slips
Within, and finds black fields and ruined towns
Where love survives on ash. Rain's in the know,

It knows we like it only from afar,
Like our own lives, if truth be told at last;
Our words stop short of rain, they miss its winks:

It asterisks a feather, stone, or stick
Then disappears, and leaves us thunder, clouds,
And obscure signs. We do not know the rain.

Gillyflower

Listening to 'Spoonful', Commonwealth Park, Summer 1976

I wanted love to touch you that warm day
Molten guitars were playing in the fire
Of a late afternoon that pinked my flesh

Your arm blonde little hairs upon your arm
Isn't it pretty you said and looked away
A dragonfly from fingertip to wrist

Was clinging to a single blade near where
You threw your bag it held the diamond world
Inside its eyes then flew off backwards yes

It's pretty said my smile oceans of air
Above us as we lay in that rich grass
Galahs high up in branches looking down

So much I wanted God so much that day
White gillyflower going to my head
Please don't release me from this flesh too soon

This melting afternoon this singing light
I wanted love to touch you there your arm
But then you moved away to wear some shade

Come back dear time I only looked aside
Pass me the spoon again but you had turned
To watch pink birds fly off towards the lake

A moment stinging worse with every year
With grief nests one two three across my world
Always that song your words beneath its chords

God looking down on me perhaps that day
Able to see it all guitars in heat
White gillies time birds flying out of sight—

The rat summons

Autun, 1522

Messieurs les rats of Autun parish, heed!
You are all summoned, from your holes and haunts,
And must attend a hearing of our court!

The charge my Lord the Bishop wants full read:
Gross gobbling of new grain and wanton wreck
Of barley fields . . . —*Ah, ça suffit, Monsieur!*

We chewed on naked grain, but did not steal
From any child's congealing bowl, or drag
A filthy crust from an unruly monk;

We smelt fresh moonlight creaming barley heads,
It made us drunk in two fast gulps of air,
And so we ran or fell or swam: we braved

Spread talons of fierce owl, raw weasel teeth.
Our God fair lit our way into a crop,
Young sunlight striding there upon his land,

And bade us eat. So put the sun on trial,
And whip it bloody in your Public Square,
Hunt down that monster lightning when it strikes

And crucify it on the tree it burns.
No devil crept in through my eyes, I swear
Upon Christ's flesh: you'll find no sweat on me.

I'll live my year out to its final scrap
And not risk knowing how a cat's fine claw
Feels in my throat. So no more words, Monsieur,

You leave your lawyers, with their falling bands,
To dine on cassoulet and burgundy.
No rat will come to Autun, I'll be bound.

Spring Wheat

Near Bury St Edmonds, Suffolk, 1961

The very shadows seemed to smell of straw
That summer of my stay: uneven beams
In both those upstairs rooms, with lumpy walls

All whitewashed just a week or two before,
And one small window looking hard at wheat.
Wide August days, each one a tall brown harp

I liked to tell myself when waking up
While sunlight shivered down our corridor.
She'd left her name out in a field, she said,

But Auntie Fay had always been, well, odd,
And as those days would have at best two chords
I listened for a third with her all day.

One afternoon we saw an adder slide
Right down from thatch in one quick pulse of green,
And Auntie held me tight as we lay there,

As we did then, our days now single chords,
Often no more than her weak breath at work
As she slipped in and out all afternoon;

She seemed to hold her life between her lips
So tightly did she purse them in her sleep—
The air too sweet and still, a little dry,

A rustling sound that swayed upon each breeze,
A combine murmuring, and always smells
Of wheat and thatch and cotton sheets and balm,

Sometimes faint whitewash from that nearby room
I never slept in, being close to her,
As I still am, when wheat dust's in the air.

New Uz

Near Sulphur, NV, 2005

You don't find many flights to Uz these days;
No call, I guess. But once upon a time
The Concorde circled like a vulture there,

And tourists streamed across paprika sand,
Fire ants beneath a pitiless pure blue.
Planes fly to Reno, though, and some rich guy

Bought what remains, and set it in Black Rock,
North East of Sulphur, as the vulture flies
(The road is sometimes there and sometimes not),

Then zipped around the globe and slowly made
An archive of all modes of suffering:
He burned a library of sighs and screams

From Egypt, Jordan, and the Holy Land,
The usual murders, rapes, and some new things—
But go and see yourself, it's worth the price.

You're gonna love the stuff he's got in there;
The 'Boils Machine' just can't be beat, my friend,
You step inside and itch from head to foot!

New Uz, he calls the place, and he's damn proud
Of those huge cedar gates air-lifted home
And that cool way he found to facelift them;

At night they swing quite shut with a small click
(The city's always trying to break out).
On oven days sometimes it rains as well,

And locals point you to the sky to see
God's fingers, slowly reaching down to earth,
Always about to touch us, but not quite.

PHILIP PORTER

The blue lady lamp

So much depends
*upo*n

the blue lady
lamp

settled in grey
dust

beside the double
bed

Reading *The Magus* in Crete

for Dorothy Porter

I am
The flute's reed
The sharp Vee
In the shakuhachi's throat
the too taut lyre string
aching to break
the frenetic high pitch of a bouzouki
weeping in Piraeus
waiting for the eight armed squid
to gnaw me with its beak

play me

Throw me to the sea
I'll return to taunt you as the Minotaur
eating virgins as a tax on your
persistent attempts
to not love
me

Pane in the glass

Like a pane of glass
Puttied into a shape
And place not of my choosing
I wait to be peered through
Smeared by chippy fingers,
Locked up and slammed
To the point of shatter
Incapable of affect just
Seen through too easily
By anyone who bothers
To peer or glance in my direction

At times I break

A transparent jigsaw
With no pattern, picture
Or the slimmest narrative
To give a clue
Just the jagged pieces
In a huddled determination
To give up nothing

my father

Life had tanned and pickled
him by the age of ten.
A hard man, with a clear
idea of right and wrong.
Love was a distant thing
to beat the emptiness
of its loss.

But now and then it spilled
out with a couple of beers
or the occasional
warmth that came with spring sun
on his cheeks, a rollie
on his lip.

urban affection

'There is something in staying close to men and women
. . . that pleases the soul well'
—Walt Whitman, 'Children of Adam'

Yes, we've just met, by accident, yet your
glance is hesitant, you mouth 'hello' at
me like a goldfish eating. We sit like
'nighthawks' in an Edward Hopper diner.

If ninety percent of our DNA
is the same as carrots, with whom, drunk, I've
talked at length, why can't you gift me a word
or just brush *my arm ever so lightly?*

As you speak I take *a mouthful of air*
as you take in mine—the exquisite
intimacy of strangers—caught stealing
chunks from each other. An urban love poem?

Perhaps, like a child's
refrain, your heart might beat in time with mine.

tanka

a breeze rustles
bamboo leaves, lifts the folds
of my kimono . . .
last night only moonlight
wrapped itself around us

Moonflower

Epiphylum oxipetalum

Under a dazzling moon an intricate star unfolds
releasing threads of perfume
to lace the darker spaces with desire
casting olfactory nets
lures prompts . . .
to bumbling insects
and to human hearts.

Awe-filled in silent worship
we savour the brief perfection
never to stand in a vase and wilt
closing with moon's ebbing light
in a deity's white death
secret beauty left to bloom
inside the mind an exquisite mystery.

Reminiscence

He and I talk as always
tangled in threads of memories.
Tears are shared for a lost love of long ago
a beauty that stole the weather from the day.
Outside a small surrender of rain
gathers in heavier drops
on the ledge above the window.
Each droplet pauses swells and strikes
the grapevine underneath.
This audible gravity strangely echoes
the old man's ponderous choice of words
from his handsome outmoded vocabulary.
He and I both note the slow selection
of each verbal jewel.
We meet each other's eye as we register the sound.
The smile erases years.

A Reluctant Farewell

This night you were there but not there.
Time passed, softly dragged like a branch across sand.
I remain held fast by memory of a special love
that defies analysis—
you have no particular beauty
your mind does not leap into the unknown
there is no fire of thought . . .
but when I think of you
I recognise something primeval
barbarously honest
older than the oceans
something emotionally genuine
that was there in the first light.
While we worked tonight you sat there
shawled in silence.
Wordless I sought connection with eyes and hands
willing songs of Circe to equip me
though constancy is an absurd notion
in a world in constant flux.
My head fills with the sad choreography
of farewells and isolation.

Love in Winter

As we approach the lodge
the densely stippled air thins slightly
before the loaded snow-cat
eddies of fine flakes whirling upwards
to stick against struggling wipers.
My fingers hum with cold.

The baggage abandoned in the rooms
we curl into chairs and lounges beside the fire.
My son and his love sit discretely entwined.
It makes me think of jasmine in the Spring
small invisible tendrils reaching and joining
at every point that offers.

There is casual easy grace in the sprawl
of long young limbs.
A tenderness squeezes my heart
into the shape of times past.
The sadness of meeting perfection in existence
is the longing to shelter it forever from change.

Regret

Steeped in high spirits
the boys unfurled laughter
and swung it about
tripping one another.

The small group surged forward
like a single mayhem unit
and rushed on the sleepy cat
beside the garden fence.

Startled to its feet
it fled along the fence line
under the pickets
and out into the street.

They shouted war cries
storming forward in pursuit
as neighbours backed from a driveway
and struck the small grey form.

The group stood still in shock . . .
one child gently lifted the ruin of the cat
saw the fragile tongue extruded
and sobbed for the end of the world.

Separation

Caught in the tide of you
your skin moving
liquid against mine
the surf of my heart
booming in my ears . . .
in this ever and never place
give me a small beacon
so that in some future
unknown space in time
I can navigate back to you
through the stars

If They Ask

If they ask
Where do I look for love?
Point to the edge of the world
To the ripples on the ocean
Swallowing the night

Love lives where mountain peaks
Sip the clouds
And rivers begin their flight

This way

If they ask
How do I know love is true?
Climb onto the roof top and dance
In every step you take
I am

If they ask
Why do I weep for love?
Let them hear the ocean cry
Let them see the stars dissolving
In your tear drops

My love has this shape

If they ask
Am I willing to die for love?
Throw off the cloak of night
Kiss my lips
And whisper the names of Life

Here on earth we circle
A secret turning
The arc of splendour burning
The sun god dripping gold into the sea

Beyond dawn
Beyond ideas and reason
I have been there

Where words have burst
And poetry quivers in a song

I'll meet you there

On this morning of freedom
You are my father, brother, lover
eagle, lion, sun, king, god . . .
You are love.

Gypsy Road Madness

When Road ran away
It turned into river
When Night ran away
It turned into star
When Dish ran away
With a sweet talking spoon
Their tryst was spectacular

When Moon ran away
It played in the shadows
When Sun ran away
It turned into light
When Wind ran away
With a twisting string theory
The rules of the world took flight

Tears ran away and turned into poem
Rhyme spilled out of a song
Life ran away with kiss and a prayer
And soon things would go terribly wrong

Song ran away
And turned into hunger
Then thunder roared through Zanzibar
Time ran away and turned into ocean
Hope ran and hid in a jar
When Love went a-riding the wraiths of the mountain
All the Gods wept for Golgotha

Dreams ran away and played in the shadows
Broken hearts yearned to be free
While the rules of the world were still waiting
For Myths to rise from the sea

The secret chord
A sliding door
Inside the Holy paradox
Behind the curtain of fixed stars
Silence whispers to the future
Destiny waits inside the past

Ophelia

A willow tree
A babbling brook
A crown of flowers in her hair

She plunges into silence
Shame and sadness now lie bare

Ophelia rides at midnight
Among the whispering of winter prayers
Weaving Hamlet in his dreaming
Through the weft and woes of meaning
Across purple moors
And scarlet shores
Of jagged silent screaming

He didst come into my bed
She whispers to the brook
Many words of love he said
And promised me to wed
But there was a madness in his look

He took my wrist and held my arm
And sighed so piteous and profound
I knew he was not in jest or joke
And I unbuttoned my night gown

On his sleeping eyelids
Did I pansies place
So he would love me in the morn
And in the arms of Love's embrace
I waited for the dawn

Here's Rosemary for remembrance
How could you forget?
Herb o' Grace will speed my prayers
And there's Rue for my regret
A secret kiss
A lovers tryst
The evening mist

A heart that breaks
A freezing lake
Then swirling, swirling
Unfurling, hurling
Whirling into the abyss

Like a mermaid she floats
Among her petticoats
Glistening like a jewel of the sea
Released from her loneliness
At last she is free

The gathering prays
On holy ground
The priest has his misgivings
But flower crowned
Drowned
Spellbound
At last her soul is heaven bound

Richard James Allen &
Benjamin Dodds

Menu

Bread / Piadina with extra virgin olive oil and balsamic
Marinated olives
Marinated grilled eggplant
Green beans with lemon
Bruschetta with tomato and grilled smoked mozzarella

❧

Risotto with zucchini, peas and herbs

❧

Tomato, cucumber, and herb salad with rocket
Roast potatoes with smoked paprika
Silver beet with lemon and walnuts

❧

John Dory fillets with a tomato, caper, olive, and herb salsa

❧

Tiny ripples mar the surface of the ocean lapping in this room
—once the abode of a child, the sanctuary of a couple, the last refuge
of a widowed great aunt—to stir from the complacency
of their long sleep those who refuse to wake.
—Richard James Allen from 'The Singing Whirlpool in the Guest Room'

Clad in khaki combat dress
and hats fur felt, with turned-down brims
an army jazz septet strikes up
Oh when the Saints, Oh when the Saints . . .
The saints may march, but the band just stomps
—Thomas Thorpe from '*Legacy* in Chatswood Mall'

My grandmother's house had a big back yard
with a long, long bench and the seats were hard;
a cage with a cocky that laid white eggs
lined on the bottom with Ginger Meggs.
—Helen Bersten from 'My Grandmother's House'

My mother's breasts were astronauts
drawn up close and high

in a latex matrix of Playtex warp and weft.
—Benjamin Dodds from 'Space Age'

Delicate Awakening

Getting me out of sleep
must be done delicately,
like raising an ancient shipwreck
slowly and in one piece
up from the seabed.

Once I am awake,
I can be present, magnificent.
But keep an eye on me,
as all my separate pieces
yearn to fold back into the sea.

Central Dreaming

it is beautiful
watching someone think
that suspended moment
halfway through a sandwich
when something about
the smile on the face
in the poster
across the tracks
is a siren call
that drags time away

and before they take their next bite
everything on the platform
seems to stop

except the ghosts
from the old Devonshire Street Cemetery
the ones who didn't move on
when their caskets were exhumed
and their bones reinterred
in cemeteries across Sydney
to construct the new
Central Station
in the early nineteen-hundreds

you can see them hanging
weighted and weightless
in the corners of the platforms
windless old winter coats
peering out from their unresolved darknesses
at the relentlessly colourful parade
of generation after generation
of newer and newer Australians
right up to the drag queen in the hijab
standing nervously next to you

everyone else stops
except the drag queen and the ghosts
who take this as an invitation to the dance

Alarming

Your alarm clock is your friend. It wrenches you out of sleep
like a pagan's fist piercing a sacrificial victim's chest
to twist out their heart. Yet on the other side of this
wakey-wakey hanky-panky lies the real sleep of horrors
if you do not wake. Out of what one could only wish to be
the heavy-lidded, azure blue sky-eyes of sleep,
where do these impenetrable night sweat storm fronts come from
and how much should you be terrified that these tornado torments
have the potential to manifest in some way
as psychometric performance tests in the non-sleeping world?

You can hardly bear to imagine what a coma would be like for you—
something like being buried alive in an underground chamber
with a whole theatre troupe of mask-sized spiders
squeezing and dropping out of cracks
that widen like grinning mouths each day in every wall,
clattering about this dungeon like the echoes of a cough
that cannot escape the darkest cavities of the lungs.

And then their ghoul faces taking on the countenances
of those you have known and trusted in your life
and almost casually spinning all around you
a sticky web of whispering lies and glancing betrayals,
until they lose themselves in their parts
and turn on each other in a pantomime of horror,
a floor to ceiling bloodbath whose acid storm feud squall
melts this entombed structure,
freeing you from your buried prison,
but drains away to expose nerve damage everywhere,

and you are left in a forest of upturned trees,
blown over by psychophysical weather events
no forecaster saw coming,
and what remains, lapping at your feet,
is every creeping crawling thing
that is worse than death,
the beastliness that is revealed
when you flip over the rock of life itself,
and all your hopes,
and everything you ever dreamed of,
float face down in the putrid pools
left by this bitter and sticky emotional rain.

Easy Difficulty

we are the unhappiness machines
assets of luminous anxieties
slowing down for the dark
nothing good has happened
since you died
buses replace strangers
half asleep most of the time
unaware that we are
curling in and out
of the unfinished business
of quantum travellers
while the birds take bets in the park
on what is the opposite of grace

The Resurrection and the Life

It seems unlikely that a few more words
will leverage me out of this wherever I am.
They don't have the force of rapture
and I am not sure that even finally
making my flying dreams real
will catch me suddenly up out of this
maelstrom of gravitational torpor.
But perhaps words are as a good a tool as any
in the truth and revelation business,
imaginary winches to haul me
out of the imaginary hole in my imaginary head,
conjured up crowbars to break open
this what feels like a tomb in which
the only part of me that is real lies buried.

The Singing Whirlpool in the Guest Room

Chased out of sleep by the ghosts of old alarm clocks,
I wonder what other guests sojourned in this room,
whether they too were drawn from their own into the dreams
of those who lay their heads on these pillows before them.

So many now in pastness.
I feel myself becoming translucent,
part of the furniture of time, the ebb and flow
of the atmosphere of what is left behind.

Yet the ringing remains
—ricocheting
from before our imaginations—

warning calls bellowed into the black
by underwater buffalo
ranging across deep sea trenches
without the need for sight.

Tiny ripples mar the surface of the ocean lapping in this room
—once the abode of a child, the sanctuary of a couple, the last refuge
of a widowed great aunt—to stir from the complacency
of their long sleep those who refuse to wake.

Chatswood Morning

Warm, cloudy, autumn day
sun fighting to break through.
I sit outside the coffee lounge
order tea and watch the busy flow
of people to and from the shops around.
Across the road: a perfume sale
you could treat a loving friend;
Shakespeare's Pies—with chips, of course,
suits on special—this week only
and banks with friendly mortgage offers.
The Sushi Bar's just round the corner
next to *Taste Our Fine Gelato.*

Mum with mobile phone and toddler
and agile thumb in conversation.
Her skipping child's so many questions
go unheard, and so unanswered.
Middle-aged couple walking slowly
hand in hand, with mauve bouquet.
Several children dodge about
mid-week—must be wagging school.
Men push strollers, carry babies
role acceptance, celebration?
Mix of faces, mix of language
reflected in shop names and signs.

All the very casual street-wear
has been chosen with much care.
Many, many mobile phones
but, girl or woman, man or boy
hardly any talkers smile.
I scan my paper—news of wars
weasel words of politicians
skinny models' fashion photos
and so-bewildering finance pages.
How unlike this local scene
of mothers, fathers, shoppers, strollers
buses, cars and mobile phones.

Legacy in Chatswood Mall

In the Mall's mid-morning crowd
idling shoppers, coffee drinkers, ice-cream eaters
wheelchair-bound *Big Issue* seller
and, for one day only, there's a soldier
and a few well-dressed civilians
bearing trays of pens and badges
all with well-rehearsed replies, to
Who is Legacy?   What is this?

Then, disturbing busy pigeons
from the shadow of a bank
comes an unexpected sound
Clad in khaki combat dress
and hats fur felt, with turned-down brims
an army jazz septet strikes up
Oh when the Saints, Oh when the Saints . . .
The saints may march, but the band just stomps.

Fronting the photo-snapping crowd
two small girls with trim top-knots
twin-like, bright Kokeshi dolls
stand spellbound and watch and listen.
This most un-military sound, ricochets around the mall
bouncing off plate glass and tiles
spreading smiles and jigs around
a rhythmic appeal for a good Aussie cause.

The Captain rocks with her clarinet
brass gives way to the banjo player
and the drums increase the power of their beat
Oh when the saints, Oh when the saints . . .
And then the trumpeter begins to sing
OH WHEN THE SAINTS   GO MARCHING IN . . .
Startled the twin Kokeshi dolls
turn and scurry back to mother.

Locomotion

High summer and the Mall is full of legs
of many lengths and widths and shapes
and in a range of colours too.
Fortunately the legs of males
are in a small minority.
It's strange how such a mechanism
designed for human locomotion
in silent, smooth, efficient motion
can vary so in eye appeal
at least to one whose legs are hidden.
Many have such graceful curves
that eyes are drawn to follow.

  While a very special few
  turn my head as well.

Sometimes at Dawn

Sometimes
in the first pale light
I lie thinking of her.
Not daydreaming, wishing
I could reach out to touch her
but remembering
her smile that arrives
as a little explosion;
how her eyes show
warmth, understanding
sorrow or anger
to fit the moment;
how her voice, face and body
all shrug to convey
disapproval at some stupidity;
and of the way she listens
so actively, encouragingly
that secrets and confidences flow
to be accepted, then held close.
And I remember
that one day next week
we'll meet for coffee.
Reassured I turn over
to slip back into sleep.

At the Bistro

a kiss
light, unexpected
teasing, revealing, loving
gift, in a sun-drenched courtyard
understanding

an embrace
mutual, secure
giving, taking, sharing
each enfolding, each close held
endearment

a caress
gentle, persuasive
exploring, lingering, arousing
delight at hands, delight of lips
tenderness

Phone Call

Nothing in particular was said
no words of great significance
passed between us down the wire
just a very cheerful 'hello'.
A complaint or two about work
and maintaining enthusiasm
a comment about the weather
and the program for tomorrow.
There were no *bons mots* to collect
no keen wit to seize and savor
no deep sentiments to share
nor advice on life and living.

       Yet the warmth in a friendly voice
       in those few minutes made the day.

Alone

Of course we are alone in the universe.
What other intelligent creature would crawl out of the slime
only to create fear, mayhem and murder?

What other fool would spend millennia morphing into a perfect killing
    machine
complete with the propaganda and lies that feed it
when we could have spent the time nurturing our young into caring
    beings,
protecting our planet from the ravages of the elements and seeking
    enlightenment?

Only we humans are mad enough to inhabit this spaceball,
chewing it up and spitting it out
while the tail lights of other galaxies are rushing away from us as fast as
    they can.

So stop your searching, SETI.
Until we can save our species and our planet
instead of seeking to inhabit others,
we don't deserve to be on the Facebook or Twitter feeds of aliens.

If you find God give him our email and phone numbers
in case he has lost them while on holiday
and ask him to forgive us our trespasses
before we destroy another world we don't deserve.

My Grandmother's House

After A.A. Milne

My grandmother's house had a big back yard
with a long, long bench and the seats were hard;
a cage with a cocky that laid white eggs
lined on the bottom with Ginger Meggs.

My grandmother's house had a long, long hall
with rooms every side and the ceilings were tall.
She had a very high bed with a mattress of down
and a lovely cupboard where she kept her gown.

She had very blue eyes and alabaster skin
because grandma never let the sun shine in.
She kept the house very, very dark
and never went down to the local park.

The scariest room in that whole big place
was outside the bathroom, not covered in lace.
Its velvet curtain couldn't have looked meaner—
yet all it covered was the vacuum cleaner!

Early Morning Rain

I hear it coursing through the gutters.
I hear it tapping on the pane.
I hear it drumming on the rooftop.
It's early morning rain.

I lie here on my pillow,
warm and cosy in my bed
and wonder if the pouring rain
is bouncing on my head.

I look out of the window
at the grey and ugly sky
and think of all the poor wet birds
who call as they fly by.

I think of all the garden blooms
which welcome this sweet rain
and then remember, damn it all,
I've left the washing on the line again!

My Imaginary Friend

She stood at the top of the mountain
and looked across to the sea.
She raised both her arms to Heaven
and said 'Lord, what to do about me?

I've spent all my life in caring
for family and friends and the like.
I've given up hours of leisure
just to make everything right.

I'd like to go dancing at midnight
with a gorgeous young man on the beach.
I'd like to go travelling to Europe
or somewhere just easy to reach.

I'd like to come home in the morning
bedraggled and giggly and drunk.
I'd kick off my shoes on the doorstep
And wake up in time for lunch.

But I'm old and I'm tired and I'm weary
And my life is approaching its end.'
And the Lord said, 'Meet me on the sand at midnight.
I'm still your imaginary friend.'

Morning Thunder

Morning thunder overhead
fills my heart with sudden dread:
all the words we never said,
all the books we never read.

As lightning forks begin to sizzle,
those crazy songs you used to whistle
echo with the petty drizzle
of the rain above my head.

Soon the wind will grow much stronger,
and we'll see the sun no longer;
soon I will begin to ponder
'what's it like when we are dead?'

Once the storm has spent its fury;
exited, like judge and jury,
it will pass into the truly
bright and cloudless skies ahead.

Then golden sun appears like magic.
For sodden earth I'll be nostalgic.
The one thing that is really tragic—
Who'll recall the lives we've led?

Regulator

Galvanised gates
lift to divide the calm
from the chaotic:
input—process—output.
On this narrow bridge
the world is out of whack.
It's like listening to a stereo
with the sound wound up
and the balance knob
turned fully left or right.

    On the bank
a fading slump of a sign
shows a black stick-figure
in the throes of the Australian Crawl
overlaid with a thick circle
bisected by an equally thick
diagonal line.
Metres from here
dangerously adolescent men
in wet sucking board-shorts
queue at the bridge to drop again
into the irrigation canal.

The sleeping surface
snares their bombs and pin-drops
from the baking sky
and drags them down
where it's gut-punch cold.

Chased by churning echoes
they become a function of
the violent process of current.

To funnel through its breathless
grip takes maybe ten seconds
          long enough to induce
a personal panic
which must be neatly filed away
before the final re-emergence
into tingling spume and
the muted whoops of brotherhood
back at the regulator
shockingly far upstream.

On Monday's school
bus they lift thin senior shirts
over awkward shoulders
to compare backs broad
and brown as hens'
eggs   lacerated by steel
from neck to crack.

Thinning our little herd

For weeks
we had Baskerville
hounds in our heads
sweeping bold arcs
through feathered darkness
at the porch lights' circle edge.
My father's too-long absence
and the distortion
of farm-night acoustics
surely exaggerated their size
but the rigid carnage we'd find
stitched to the morning's frozen
grass did little to lessen unease.
A man who was not our father
barked stark instruction
at my brother and me:
foolproof steps
for burning a gutted calf.

The spiders are here

Last night, a sprawled grey one
planted its hugeness by the front door.
The wet outburst of its kernelled abdomen
was necessary. Once they're in,
there's no putting them out.

And today, the black economy
of a furled umbrella nestled itself in miniature
beneath the latch of the garden gate.
A creased bank statement made a neat streak of it.

Vigilance
or soon the swaying needle-rise
and drawbridge-drop of two leading legs
mount the mattress summit
to plant nightmare's waking flag.

Prodigal Son (and his partner)

A city boyfriend
when taken to stay with parents
in rural Queensland
must be made to feel
it's normal and neighbourly
to step in and out
of nearby paddocks at will.
It's customary to laugh
at his ignorance of barbed wire
and the methods of rendering it benign
by lifting or lowering its strands.
Looping a gate's galvanised chain
back upon itself and over
the mushroomed stay
must be done whilst speaking of
something entirely unrelated,
such should appear the second nature
of gate administration
in a boy born and bred on the land.
After the well-timed peach of sunset is
photographed and declared to be gorgeous,
the homeward path should take in views
of whomever's herd. And when they stamp,
lower horned heads and begin to follow,
smile knowingly at his sweet
uneasiness—they're only cows—
whilst shepherding him over the fence
by the most direct route possible.

Space Age

My mother's breasts were astronauts
drawn up close and high

in a latex matrix of Playtex warp and weft.
They manufactured the moon suits

(Playtex, not my mother's breasts)
to swaddle men against silent death.

Twenty-one layers of failsafe stitching—
cascading redundancy

made vacuum-tight by hand
under the brief

that space is equilibrium.
No blood or breath

or saliva out there;
given the chance

the void takes its share.
I'm told I screamed each time

like depressurisation
at their smothering press

and just like those gods of Apollo
had to be fed powdered milk.

Surrogacy

It is the stork who labours
to deliver baby Dumbo to his sad
and silent single mother.

The heft of a hundred-kilo sack
had to be held aloft across the Technicolor
map of Disney's pre-war USA

in search of a moving target—
a humping caterpillar of travelling circus train.
Only a domestic flight,

but imagine the sweet relief
at unlocking his beak, the tension
headache born of bearing an elephant child.

He does his job with a smile,
offers genuine warmth in generous addition
to the contractual requirement of professionalism,

congratulates the long-lashed lady
and relaunches on monochrome wings.
His total screen time is maybe three minutes,

a seasoned bit player,
agent of plot progression,
class act who only weeps in transit.

Robyn Rowland & Alex Skovron

Menu

Bread / Piadina with extra virgin olive oil and balsamic
Marinated olives
Roasted peppers
Grilled zucchini
Bruschetta with sautéed mushrooms and parmesan

❧

Risotto with pumpkin and sage

❧

White bean, tomato, and herbs salad with rocket
Green beans with lemon
Roast potatoes with rosemary

❧

Lemon and thyme marinated roasted chicken

❧

Gelato
Banana and caramel cake with crème anglaise

❧

Ardent evening stills with cicada song,
asphalt molten, a swelter of viscous past,
bridges and railings scorched bone-white,
rim sand rusting in the late-light.
—Robyn Rowland from 'Sliver of Australian Summer'

The geologist flows
around my life
like lava,
molten grey embers
that break vermilion
—Erina Booker from 'Igneous'

a peripatetic man in conceit
filling a suit and tie
as if a balloon large enough
to carry the weight
of a crisis.
—Pam Morris from 'News, as if'

A scheme for free tertiary education
I found beneath a sausage roll and Fanta
Lying in a bin beside the station.
—Stephen Mason from 'Free Education'

The man who just passed my café window
dropped his shadow accidentally
and walked on. It lies on the speckled pavement,
squirming awkwardly, unable to move. Wait.
—Alex Skovron from 'Dropped Shadows'

Stone Child

Monument to the Martyrdom of Children, Łódź, Poland.
Inscribed: Let pass to future generations our common cry:
never again war, never more camps.

It could be anywhere but it's Łódź. A heart cracked open
eight metres high, The Broken Heart Monument.
Beside it, the naked body of a scrawny boy stands emaciated.
Spine a cord of knots, head bald, his spare shadow
tunnels through her heart like a birth canal.
So high, a real boy only reaches the top of his leg,
his posture captures grief, loss, acquiescence.

At dark, you see the night sky through the gap,
weeping elms, the school that borders the park.
Here, once, two children's camps locked-in hope.
Detention of the Polish young from all over,
even Vienna. Aged two to fifteen, Jewish, Roma
or not, parents missing or dead or
suddenly in prison, confused or in resistance.

And camp two for the *germanisation* for *nordic types*
Aryan-looking enough to be sent to Germany for adoption.
But children over sixteen were adults, sent to Auschwitz, Birkenau.
Twelve thousand, possibly twenty passed through these two camps,
sixteen hundred lived here. Food short, all kinds of ravaging
took place. Six hundred survived flogging, working to death,
typhus. The ill, still living, were trucked to the morgue.

Maria Jaworska (no. 501) recalls ten-year-old Teresa Jakubowska
beaten under cold water for bed-wetting, dying three days later,
death recorded as tuberculosis. Like others, decades after the war
Zofia Kowalewska (no. 5963) fears anyone who looks at her.
The stone boy leans his head toward the massive sculptured heart,
its only likeness to the one that loved him, is the empty
space of his shape that marks his absence.

Sliver of Australian Summer

Coral-smudged runnels of thought
cross the mind of blue sky,
the loveliness of moment,
moon part-melted,
smell of water from a paddock
below the wind turbine
shocked still by heat.

Ardent evening stills with cicada song,
asphalt molten, a swelter of viscous past,
bridges and railings scorched bone-white,
rim sand rusting in the late-light.

Dragonflies herringbone the dusk
too heat-weary to mate, frenzy sucked dry.

Car windows down—I think
air-con too distancing—
strappy summer dress hunched up,
and the draught from the speed
blowing kisses on my neck, upper back,
bare except for the incandescent stroke of day.

Hero Unmasked

for my father, September 2014

We watched old back and white movies on tv
Sunday afternoons in our fifties lounge-room as kids,
ate dark chocolate with sickly green peppermint filling
running over our fingers from blocks that Pop
brought down from Sydney as a special treat.
You loved westerns—*come onnnn the Indians* you'd shout.
It was a ritual. It was family.
We devoured the forties and fifties like sugar.
Man in the Iron Mask appeared in our musketeer craze.
Here was Heroism, Love, Life and Death.

To a man rarely sick, radiotherapy was incomprehensible.
They wrapped your face in cling wrap first
to block eyes and nose tight. Built up layers of
wet Plaster of Paris to shape a mask.
I watched you struggle like the fish we'd caught,
remembered clearly the day my brother and I
wriggled you down the boat ladder in Fiji over a reef way out,
your grandkids fluttering along the surface then diving,
two sleek seals, deeper and deeper, snorkel bubbles
erupting through the meniscus of sea.
Turning I saw your frantic dog-paddle, your urgent scratching,
desperate to get back on the boat, lack of breath a broken line to life.
We heaved you back on board where you gulped at air, floundering.
You just couldn't breathe through your mouth.

In the radiation chamber I saw your body arch in panic,
rushed in, talked you through breath after breath.
I told them—'he won't be able to do it every day for six weeks.
When the mask was set next day, it was chunky, sightless—
two nose plugs erect, a strange jelly-fish splayed across your face.
Under it a mesh helmet gripped your face, Spiderman's web

clipped into place, locking your head to the bed, immoveable.
They simply said—'breathe through your mouth.'
Panic sucked the room clear of air.
I gripped your hand, watched that chest squeeze hard.
You said—'I have to find a way.'

Best part of it all was sitting on your deck at home, watching
the ocean change, birds fill your grevillea and callistemon
with wild colour—rainbow lorikeets, crimson rosellas, honeyeaters –
the simple brown sparrows that fed with you at breakfast,
pelicans overhead in their graceful jumbo flights.
You spent each morning like this—'bird watching' you called it—
and laughed—'the birds watch us!' And you found your way.
There, with poetry singing in your head, you started to recite
the old lines of Paterson, Lawson, Kendall, and I'd stumble through,
a small kid's shadow after her daddy's long strides.
Word-for-word perfect you were.

Each session at the hospital you'd recite to make yourself breathe—
lips never silent while the machine whirred,
telling the walls the wonderful poems you grew me up on.
You'd come out and say—'I got through *Clancy of the Overflow,*
The Last of his Tribe and *The Bush Christening.*'
Or 'I fitted in Bellbirds—I think they took longer this time',
and we'd drive to the harbour for coffee and cake
while I churned that you had to face anything mortal like this.
The radiology team said they'd never seen anything like it.
Of course not! They'd never met my father before—
the d'Artagnan, the Robin Hood, the Ivanhoe—of Wentworth Street!

Known by heart

Her skin chronicles his touch throughout the years—hands long-fingered,
     strong and
vellum-soft, once unspotted by age. Luminous, they held her face,
tracing that forbidden pathway in the dark under his Abbey walls.

Tender with longing—restraint—they picked for her that wild pink rose,
walking above the Glen of Aherlow twelve years into a longer good-bye.

They gestured like fluttering doves, pointing out a white swan
nesting on a lake's island, a grey heron beside it
watching, guarding—two companions so unmatched.

Hands praying a lifetime of prayer, bound his body into the swaddling
of surplice, delivered wine and wafer, married others together for life.

Years pass faster than water runs across her wrist. Yet still his fingers
always twist his greying hair as he talks, eyes lightning-blue smile in
mock-teasing, and her heart flinches to find these simple things still endear.

After thirteen years those palms held her naked, trembling, a skin-magic
love makes, burning along the abiding thread that holds her to him.

Impossibly out of time—love like that. Slowly his hands grew older
practised in rituals of denial. Awaiting surgery their ligaments contracted
to a right-hand claw, placid, white-cold as he cast her adrift.

Or so it seemed. Though never certain of the unattainable they wanted,
caged by rules that never concerned her, they were life to him, chosen, re-chosen.

And yet—meeting thirty years on, his grasp is warm in celebration, that
split from each other as the times demanded, they can still walk
Coole Park together sharing the stroke of trees shady-green along their lips.

The Dead

He watched the boy's brain leak away,
stared directly into his eyes only.
Thousands lay before him out there
where brutal harvest cut them.
Everywhere here was crowded
with the dead. The Imam sighed—
surely it was not intended,
so many children of God dead.
His clothes were stained with blood
where he held them. Thick now,
 his whole sense of cleanliness lost.
Without water, it was not possible.
There was no time to wrap them,
no white cloth, no space to lay them
in any soft earth. He scarcely believed it.
It grieved his heart that this respect
was not possible. It hurt his very bones.
His mouth was turning sour with it.

'Father,' his voiceless prayer, 'help me.'
But the priest could not carry him any further,
laid the bleeding orderly down.
He had given mass that morning in the trenches.
They were shaking and pleading for it.
He hoped it was enough for the thousands
whose last rites were unspoken
as they rushed straight into the shafts of
bayonets, the shred of bullets,
broken bodies a carpet over the land.
He could not see a grass blade.
He watched Chaplain, Hindu, Jew, bewildered.
It pained him in his chest. A knife there.
It simply cannot have been meant by God,
this wasteful slaughter. Helpless in despair
he tried for burials, but there was no stopping
a second time. It blurred the lines between
friend and enemy. As if God would define.

When he was young, once

She only knew his body when it was young.
Not this.
He rode wild horses, tamed everything, everything.
He prayed, or not.
He swept her into life.
His urgency was for her alone
not some idea of history, some vision of a hero.
Now this short year that seemed so long—
and she did not know this body now.

Not this.

Scarred, the leg gone, mind altered beyond
his being able to speak of it except to say—
'we did things we had to do'.
She had been so hungry. No food.
She had been so alone.
Everything changing, family dispersed,
confusion, no-one to underpin
all that was familiar, known.
She wanted him back.

Not this.

She only knew his body as husband.
She remembered the moustache they laughed about,
her lace veil trailing, her hennaed hands in his,
her happiness, certainty of a future—
never years passing apart, the place falling to dust,
death lists, the fear of news, the understanding
everything had gone now that she knew.
Everything changed.
She didn't want this.

Not this.

What country is this? Men full of strange energy
they call 'war'. They call 'necessary'.
She can see it in a trapped kind of way, that necessity.
But every young man from her town,
every station hand, every merchant in the market,
every father who had seemed so old then.
Now him. Old while young.
She wanted him back, real as the rocks and the sand,
lonely for the 'him' she knew in her heart, in her very loins.

Not this

From Quaternary, I–VIII

1.Dust to Dust

The geologist walks on the land
stone and rock
sing in his bones;
among kin
he knows the names—
his family tree
back to
prehistory;
Jurassic, he says,
Triassic,
Ordovician

how they wore each other out

More intimate
is the laying on
of hands—
broad, capable,
gnarled nuggets
coloured like the earth
he feels
he rubs
he may even, then,
taste

integrate

He strides hills
in his seven-league boots—
the ground swells
and buckles
around—
mounds of breast
clefts of valley;
he reads
the shapes
the fractures
and knows
what lies
beneath;
he is
omniscient

prescient

The geologist
covers the land
hundreds and thousands
of kilometres
is easy
in his element;
the ground purrs
beneath him

reciprocates

His hardness is
one to ten
on Moh's scale,
from the talc of his skin
to his diamond precision;
minerals mingle
with an alluvium of thought
a moraine of experience;
his knowledge—
sedimentary,
his passion—
igneous,
himself—
metamorphosed

complete

The geologist endures
Omnipresent—
he ceases
with the Earth.

IV. Igneous

The geologist flows
around my life
like lava,
molten grey embers
that break vermilion

he creeps over all before him
into each chink
each crevice
forcing himself between
the smallest spaces

his sweet breath
laden with
hot nothings

this could be
Pompeii

erupting magma
is unstoppable
and I am poised,
positioned,
unable to flee
there is nowhere to go

nearly 'set in stone'—
it's just a matter of Time

hope floats
soft as pumice
and equally crushable
though I am cooling now,
nearly an artefact
a has-been

in a frozen pose
dictated by conditions
events
slowly decaying
rebuilding the Earth

perhaps I will be
an archaeological find
my bones gently dusted
with brushes

wonderment at
my rigid horror

positioned
at the whim
of my surrounds

there was no choice.

VII. Fissure

You left the San Andréas fault in me
though it was never my fault
or my responsibility
now I need to
realign
redesign
redefine
and resign myself
to this
great change
rearrange
seems so strange
I'm full of
edges
ledges
cracks and splits
and mosaic bits;
Perhaps the Canyon
or the Great Divide
cut up inside
no place to hide
both sides apart
losing heart
I'll never be
a work of art—
it was such a
vicious fissure
under pressure.

Icon

so we made your last-wish trip
right into the Red Centre
the country of belonging
where spirit sings in your bones
and light splits into pure spectrum colours
from red dirt to violet rocks

I'm still living this
though you are not,
photos tumble from phones
as startling as spiders
from a drainpipe:
a deluge of memory
that bends me in two

and now this print is framed
gold dingoes
red dirt
Kata Tjuta
with its *a cappella* chorus
violet on the horizon,
another relic

I hold it firmly against me
and all I can think is
'I got you, babe.'

Ariadne's Lament

I admit
we both had
hidden agendas

though I looked best
finally
when you abandoned me

a maze of expectation
which perhaps
amazed you

as your intention
was only towards
the Minotaur

and my appearance
though timely
caused you

to lose
the thread
of your story

you walked away
not from the Minotaur without
but from the Minotaur within

I make no sound;
who ever hears?

The Turning of the Leaves

I have answered
with Spring
time and again,
the swell of sap
the green effusion;

and then
like a time-lapse image
I have answered
also
with conflagrations
of colour:
fiery pyres
of scarlet, maroon, cerise,
and the unexpected
peach;

now it's time for peace—
my years
clustered
like snow,
my hair
fragrant
from leaf smoke,
ashy
from burned bridges.

Every six weeks—the hairdresser

The cloth is light, silky,
a red wave on my body
to catch my hair as it falls
and scatters, white on red.

A cluster of leaves blown
by a fretful wind and then
a flock of birds taking off
to fly against the sky.

My every-day bag holds
my name and address,
my cards and coins, a pen,
my next appointment.

It is covered in tapestry
of coloured flowers, red,
pink, blue, and a butterfly
amongst wild grasses.

Birds will be startled,
and there'll be a wind when
we go to your funeral:
you went so suddenly.

Left ear audio

A guitar and a voice sing the sound of a song, 'Waves of Joy',
after a program on the science of String Theory at 3 o'çlock
on a Tuesday afternoon two days after the last hot Sunday.

The persuasive and enthusiastic physicist says String Theory
is about everything we can or cannot see, and could be the sum
of it all except, he says, it can't be proven: the quantum leaps

and algorithms don't add up to a provable sum which, in my sleepy state,
awash on the strains of 'Waves of Joy', was a comfort to hear before
the 4 o'clock news. Sufficient for me to gather all the parts of myself

which had melted into an almost sleep, a realm of dreams and waves
and other distant connections, enough for me to recognise again
this bed, this floor, that leaf and sunfilled window, that ordinary door,

that passage to the garden and the centre of this small cottage
on a suburban street in Willoughby, NSW. At school I would add:
Australia, the World, the Universe, but today we can't help but know

we are in the Milky Way among all the other galaxies where, in the midst
of our troubled grounding we're told our bits and pieces, our eyes, lips,
fingers, our ordinary tumbling feet, our lives, our loves, our history trails

of who and when—our dust—will eventually be out there as stars,
or vibrating strings jazzing, harmonising all over in the lower and upper
atmospheres waiting for a theory to catch up. Our street, like many,

goes up and down, a man hurries past, a girl heads home, there are eleven
dimensions all around, a post box and a bus stop on the corner and
tomorrow, if I am ready soon after breakfast, I will catch the bus to town.

News, as if

Problematic air hangs around,
moves as he enters,
waits for the opportunity
to rush in as his lips form
an aperture.

Fingers on a lifted hand
curl to a point
and let fall a paradox:

a peripatetic man in conceit
filling a suit and tie
as if a balloon large enough
to carry the weight
of a crisis.

some cloud

That cloud, heavy with rain, hangs overhead
in the window of the late blue sky softening
to pink in the southwest over the olive dark trees
and the distant city; changeable, something like

waking in the morning not knowing what day will bring:
happenings, messages, lifted pavements, ordinarily
straight and flat as pavements go yet not, as the cloud box
in the forecast would tell us, true. Rain may come,

or there will be sun with some cloud, here where my two feet
have walked me over ups and downs and, through the limber
of my body discerned right and left, not always well,
dissembling sufficiently to bring me here today.

Who could have foretold the fine trace of pen on paper,
the foot directing, the eye perceiving, the hand committing.

Tawny frogmouth

Look again in the midst of a tall tree—something?
A shift, a shape? Old wood? Leaves turn and change
and, like the sea caught in a small wind, you are there

but not there. Alive, dead? Ah, a bundle of feathers,
dissembling, obfuscating, pretending. Brindled
grey, red, silver, mottled as my feelings.

I pay attention and you are an owl, yellow eyes
above a beak, quietly watching me. This is what I feared
might come, something I could not know, seek out, defy.

I turn away. You are beautiful, your soft feathers stir
as you rest. You have no business with me yet
you are a harbinger, indeterminate, torn. It may be

you are named frogmouth, a comical screen,
but you are not a frog, and your beak is sharp. Now
you are discovered there, remain while I tell you

words from my mouth can charge argument, encounter.
Owl, dear frogmouth, I will speak here in these lines, black
on the page, direct as the pupils of your yellow eyes,
I cannot help but see you as yourself, but written otherwise.

PAM MORRIS

The other day

Red, pink, blue and green
some way ahead
walking downhill slowly.

From his shoulder, a black bag,
in her hand, a white one.
I could see her dark hair
and the pale round
behind the curve of his ear.

A few steps on,
just near the myrtle tree
ready to flower,
she nudged her shoulder to his
and their arms moved
for an easy exchange of bags,
white to him, black to her.

I couldn't see their faces
but I'm sure, on a slight turn
and a flicker of eyes,
there was a glance
of quiet affection.

Hamlet's Defeat

port arthur of course our first off-shore facility
our first people smugglers being
staunch english governors

to be a con or not to be a con artist's history

jesus was murdered in custody,
saint paul john pat eddie murray . . .

you frightened boat people
who come here for solace
who want to share our claudian stolen liberty

in apprehension how like the christian god
we nail you off-shore to manus and nauru

Recycling Trashed Song

oh sonnet litter fourteen lines long
you're in the trash with me crazy blind
deaf and dumb recycling dumpstered song
discarded muse from history's bin your kind
seductive shape of gorgeous rhyme so fine
your word a whispered kiss in perfumed lace
I can't resist your crisp mature wine
I take your measured skipping sweet embrace
to heart. We do the twist around the stars
in winds of constellation spin. We bowl
their circling stairs through strobe-lit midnight bars.
oh dinosauring sonnet comet roll
me over supernova strike your note
and take me down I drown to float your boat

Free Education

A scheme for free tertiary education
I found beneath a sausage roll and Fanta
Lying in a bin beside the station.
Not prepared for academic banter
Going nowhere, I took the sausage roll
And left the essay in a pool of sauce.
I found a bench seat next to where a doll
Was talking on her phone about a horse.
I peeled the pastry off the sausage finger,
Wrapped some cheese around it like a bandage,
Watched a busker play guitar, a singer
Sing flamingo songs in Spanish language.
Education's always free to me.
This class of Barcelona morning tea.

Song 23

I don't know how to look out this
window but to story time

I don't know how to share this
crepe suzette of mumbled dreams

except the wind is nudging me
except the sea is calling me   to swim

so words flow, the sky falls
leaves colour the day breaks
till all is broken crumbs
of the perfect verb
        on the perfect wave
birds drift this smoky song
through lost names so redescribed this
history is renewed

and how the horses stare
how the river never leaves
how the music weaves its lilt
into the voices on the stairs

like a whispered crepe suzette
like the story of a window

all adrift with birds on the perfect wave

Crowded Café Psalm

1

this open harbour with its rivers and beaches
coffee with croissant or blueberry smoothie
ferry trip to manly train along the hawkesbury
in all our pop bland or sensational fashion

this city by the sea bondi cliff-walk to coogee
brisk walkers sporting startled hair and glittered jeans
through all the streets of surry hills newtown glebe

streaming jacaranda yawn
from balcony to back laneway

cyclists passing stalling rows
of banked up morning traffic horns
on roads lined with planted plots
of stark purple fountain grass

café queues for egg on vegied
smashed avocado toast
slouching out on paths strewn
with scattered frangipani flowers

so crowds come and go out of streets into parks
across traffic from shop to buffalo grass
lights spilling fountain shadows through water
fleeting hair and darting eyes rushing into the bright arcade

2

we shop the fizzling wine show of fading love, shopped,
returned, lost, restored, in stray talk of him or her
who made a start at love and then so

casually broke the broken heart again it seems
we may find hope slowly sipping
whipped romance between the coffee and the cream
where all the people live and talk and stream
from home to work and out   I sit and write quietly
as the froth of Disney on the rocks
from Donald Duck to Donald Trump
crashes all around me here at the feet of tall liberty's dreams
screening yankee morning news across the fabled land of oz
into our cafés by the sea or in the bluesy mountain tops
I order another cup and write these crowded notes
among waterfalls flowing into jingles and chocolate soap

(and I know I hear you calling
in this silence that is falling
on mount zalmon in my heart

cascading down the mountain of your psalms into the sea)

like a vocation to anonymity
I am lost in the waters of the crowd to find my voice
among people milling out along the sand in bare feet with dogs
stepping into sudden economic headwinds
from casinos drowning in seventies' songs

we sit and watch breakers rising in the sun, as,
irascibly independent
of reasonable explanation
you make yourself the event
of the moment in the poem

then disappear back into the beauty of creation
this open harbour with its rivers and beaches
coffee with croissant or blueberry smoothie

Bondi

i.m. Graeme Thorne

Almost the week the boy
was taken away, we moved in—

Edward Street was on the news,
police came and went.

He had been tricked into a car
outside a corner grocery

just down the street. Strange
to think now of that

Four Square Store, and of him
hurrying towards it

to his fate—the very shop that
I, leaping off the bus

in years to come, would visit
for an after-school licorice stick

or Nestlé's sixpenny-thin
chocolate tile (an aircraft card

inside each); the shop where
I, descending Wellington Street

in years to come, would turn
left into O'Brien Street,

walk another block, and there
await by the rickety fence

the School Special to Randwick,
watching for the latest cars,

schoolbag grounded, and safe
between my shoes

Dropped Shadows

'If a problem is stated in the wrong terms,
it cannot be solved.'
—Czesław Miłosz

The man who just passed my café window
dropped his shadow accidentally
and walked on. It lies on the speckled pavement,
squirming awkwardly, unable to move. Wait.
A girl being dragged by an anxious mum
has also just let her shadow fall. Half-hearted,
she looks back at the shimmering shape
still twisting on the concrete, but allows herself
to be tugged along without protest, after
a final furtive backward glance. I ask myself:
if I drained my macchiato, stood up and stepped
outside, would I too discover my shadow
slipping from me? How does one deal with
the loss of one's shadow? A preposterous notion,
I must be imagining things—
                           Wait! It's happened
again, to the greengrocer across the street,
arguing with some kid outside his shop.
I'm certain I saw his shadow slither down
onto the sidewalk, it rests there trembling
in its own darkness. The sun has just retreated
behind a cloud—I'm going to leave
this café before that sun comes out again.
I don't trust myself to stay whole anymore.

Arcane Geometry

'Where is the truth of unremembered things?'
—Czesław Miłosz

It is the unremembered things which harbour truth;
    things forgotten and things pushed past forgetting,
that surface suddenly in the creak of a gate
    at sunset, or jolt us out of a dream of forbidden cellars
where our first kiss went untasted, rooms
    where we whispered nothing and the night alone
witnessed the contours of our febrile silence.
    Admit that the hazy outline of the staircase down into
the deep decades is beyond your grasp,
    it quivers there, just across the chasm of a thought;
confess that no truer note calls from the gone seasons
    than that pulse of longing somewhere so near, almost
audible—behind, within—each time you cross
    the open quadrangles and shadowed cloisters that turn
your imaginings into daguerreotypes
    of unrequited fancy, warm velleities or cooling hopes
that refuse to surrender their essence which is
    your essence. How often has a song requickened
from a car radio ancient pleasures abandoned or unknown,
    or carved abruptly a channel into childhood's
helpless diligence, transforming the moment
    into a truth that is yet impossible to reshape
into the touchable, a clue from some arcane geometry
    whose angles you cannot decipher no matter how you
strain to translate its axioms into legible script?
    Where, then, is that which, long dead, is yet alive
but irrecallable, barely glimpsed, forever blanketed
    under the fathomless cloak of the past? And when
will there come a chance to snatch at that cloak,
    expose the outlines and contours of the elusive psalm

beneath?—To confront at last the true trace of time,
      the unremembered things that wait quietly
inside the dusty almanacs of our desires?—To strip away
      the illusions we employ a lifetime to tend and cultivate
while the truths we do remember wither in the hothouse
      we inhabit?—To reveal the forgotten garden
that flourishes somewhere there, among the shaded beds
      and hidden furrows of what we mistake for ourselves?

Visitation

At one point, exhausted from pilgrimage,
we ceased exploring the drowsy churchyard
because I wanted a photograph of you
standing at the centre of the ruined transept
of this relic from the Wars of the Roses;
but just as the shutter clicked, you squinted
toward the skyline, disturbed by a muted drone
that became a glinting speck high in the west
and shimmered to a flying machine—one
of those biplanes we could both remember
from before the war, one very like a Tiger Moth
father had hoisted me into somewhere
deep among the lost paddocks of the past,
deep among all the dimmed remembrances
of a childhood whose measure had been flight,
from one home, one school to the next,
in pursuit of a future we never found; and here,
now, this visitation, and I began to re-imagine
that summer's day, an old barn burning
beside the airfield, my first ice-cream, father
handing me gently into the tall cockpit
I had so yearned to conquer, mother, unsure,
hovering on the periphery . . . But as I drifted
aboard the memory of that morning, the plane,
by now almost precisely at our zenith,
gave out a choking stutter, stalled, and plunged,
in a silent beautiful spiral, into a copse
on the far side of the ridge above the church;
you clamped a palm to your mouth, but I
could only stare as the plume crawled upward,
heavenward, black as an afterthought.

Serenade

From the terrace next door there rises this frothy serenade—
they're spinning their 78s again, the needle drags, any moment now
  the old boxer in the downstairs yard will commence his infernal howling:
he's been somewhat more pugnacious of late, easily enraged,
  forever ready to nip at passing keisters. Not that there's too much traffic
here these days, except for all those dirty little hooligans of a Friday,
  spilling their grubby trannies at top volume, smooching and grabbing
under the Moreton Bays, or playing this peculiar hide-and-seek.
  'Ready coming or not!' they yell from the lane next to Parasol's garage,
which hasn't seen a customer in years (they say he's just keeping it
  for the taxman). Yup, there goes Rocky again—our classical neighbours
can't abide the brute, complain that he's always bothering their music.
  Well, I'm not impartial to the classics myself, but *I* reckon
it's the other way round! They actually called the cops the other night:
  after an hour, this phlegmatic sergeant with a scrawny sidekick
(ready to start shaving any day now) pulled up behind old Jock's removal van.
  I couldn't really say what transpired, I was over at Murphy's at the time
and heard it second-hand; but you can bet they grouched all the way
  back to the station – a pretentious little deco bungalow that could do
with a coat of paint. Virgil upstairs just tossed an orange at Rocky.
  You might as well hitch a horse to a Holden!

Legend

But this was 1969: her father seemed so old that
I expected him to crumple at any moment. Instead he folded

his fat Saturday paper, smiled Nixonically
and, thoughtful, brushed at his shadow like an alcoholic. 'We

eat at six on Saturdays, you're welcome to join us.
In the meantime, drive nicely.' At last: we were alone as

a couple of cosy parkers in Lovers' Lane, or almost—this was a
daytime date so we'd have to make do. And because her

Psych project was due Monday, and tonight being the night of
her babysitting debut, most of the weekend was a write-off.

So we drove down to this windy deserted beach
halfway along the coast, to a place where they'd converted each

little picnickers' bay into a sheltered virtually one-car
niche, turned off the wipers, the motor, managed to plunk our

starving bodies into the back, where, peeking over at
me like a magnet she loosened herself somewhat and 'Gopherit!'

she said. And before we knew it, as the cross-hatched rain
sealed us into our great dream forever, latched in our hot pain

against the wet world, half-naked where it mattered;
and as I watched her effigy unveil, and our teeth chattered

in the steam of the afternoon downpour, and she unravelled a
hand into my skin, and I sensed her perfect shadowy parabola

remould itself and disappear somewhere and grow ample,
and understood the thrall of Samson as he grasped the temple

pillars with all his love and all of his power; and as I knew all
this, I suddenly recalled, absurdly, that the fuel

gauge had been sitting on absolute zero and in a while I'd
have to restart the car; I thought of her dry old dad and I smiled,

and I looked into her spinning, half-open eyes and her arms clung
irreleasably and that was the moment I drowned, there among

the pounding waves of rain and her infinite lips . . . That and
the radio humming, and 1969; and who cares today if any of this

is anywhere near the way it never quite happened.

Kit Kelen & Iggy McGovern

Menu

Bread / Piadina with extra virgin olive oil and balsamic
Marinated olives
Roasted eggplant
Roasted Pumpkin
Bruschetta with white beans, rosemary and parmesan

❦

Risotto with cauliflower, parsley and parmesan

❦

Rocket, pear and parmesan salad
Cavalo nero
Roast potatoes with smoked paprika

❦

Roast beef with seeded mustard

❦

Gelato
Chocolate cake with chocolate sauce

❦

embrace the poem
squander the soul
sleep to dream and wake to play
let everything go wild today
—Kit Kelen from 'let everything grow wild today'

We must do something drastic,
We must now take a punt,
Lest the whole English language
Is reduced to a grunt!
—Mickey Millner from 'Sesquipedalian'

How far between heaven and hell.
The blink of an eye,
a lifetime.
Where do you sit in this diorama?
—Julie Fredericks from 'Untitled'

And in the hall a girl slinks by
As I write poetry on my phone.
She winks
and asks if I'm a Gemini
I ask if she's alone.
—Gary McCartney from 'Dreaming of the New Camden'

When I shared a bed
in nineteen fifty-two or three
with my bony father, I was led
to believe that we
were alone;
—Iggy McGovern from 'Bony'

let everything grow wild today

embrace the poem
squander the soul
sleep to dream and wake to play
let everything go wild today

let the spirits call our names
let us requite

only the words
to bear

from my door
nowhere but the way

everything green is reaching for heaven
for light and for love

squander the paint
set afloat in a poem

only words
to be borne
to bear on

let everything go wild today
wake to play and sleeping dream

so we may work the miracle
set God and godly things
all free

today
let everything grow wild

practical hypothetical

follow a rule
until it's broken

when you've gone too far
go on

just for example
take truth on its toes
peering up over the top of the wall
to see if a hunch was right

Blokes

Blokes are always coming over, in their droves
or in their ones. Wear thongs in summer, boots
for weather. No one says mind my clean floor love.

Arriving in their utes and vans, they're always
round here, day and night, courting our Penelope.
They know what's next, what's what, when, why.
Blokes know what to do and what you need
and even if you can't decide. Blokes'll sort your
trouble out. If it aint broke it's easy fixed. Take
care but not responsible. They're always late
and rude and wet. Blokes like to be outside
the best. They dare the ozone at their backs.
Sleep with someone else. They say things you
wouldn't. Feel less, do more. You've got to love
them though. Hide in their frothy beards to weep.
You feel for them, the camera shies. They won't
be tied, won't be predicted. But cuddle them
and know they're bad. Take them all for granted.

Blokes won't take hints. Needn't tell them.
They slink away to shed when glum. Grow darker
in the moody scrub and shed their lacks among
the fauna. They won't be caught, they get away.
Get down to pub and dob and dob, until they're
almost in the clink. They tell their temporary
comrades. Blokes tell the truth and when they
don't they've got the story all worked out.

They know the pecking order. How to fit, not rock
the boat. Blokes make a play for the affections.
Trust the passing moment, loathe permanence
of plans. Blokes are slaves of circumstance. They
can't help being rough with stuff, have to give it
all a test. See if it's well made or not. It's not
their fault the way they are, was done
to them as blokelings.

Blokes are mates or so they say. Won't let
a bastard down. The blokiest are your best mates.
Your mates are blokes if you're a bloke. Women
can be mates or ladies. Can't be blokes. Mate
with them to make new playmates. Blokes or no.
If you're a bloke you mustn't mate with other
blokes. It doesn't work. Dreadful thing.
Unblokemanlike. Besides, how could
you tell your mates?

Some things are better left unsaid. And out of
earshot of the nagging blokes won't need
your looking after. Dinners tabled, washing done.
Blokes go lean in filth and glue their rotting jeans
together. They know it's bad luck to speak
when gesturing would do the trick.

As insects lead the faster life, they've lost a leg
before you've finished telling the precautions.
They're enemies of labour saving, scoff at
ingenuity. Do a thing the hardest way. Clog noses
and their ears fall off, eyes are full of filings.
Drown in beer to build a gut. It shows what
blokey blokes they are. They suffer beef to have
the dripping. Sneak from the ward at last
for fags, and curse their curtailed freedom.
That's with a final breath.

Bloody this and bloody that is what your bloke
ghost says at last. And when the dirt's all spread,
well sifted—where are those blokey souls all fled?
They've gone to blokeland—hellish spot. The
Shed Celestial. Dim or Bright to their deservings.

Still, there's more. Never was a drought of blokes.
Not since the war. No—blokelings grow to
blokehood's full bloom. Bloke's abound and pull
their weight. Show some leg, offer beer.
Call for blokes—they will appear.
When all else fails no need to fear.
Just stir him up. Your bloke is here.

Magyar idyll

my ancestors are burning
across an endless steppe
somewhere out of Asia
they harry the poor and the weak
                    on their way
they're torching the lowlands
they're putting an axe to the forest
they're making the Great Hungarian Plain
the woodland creatures they turn into *gulacs*

of course I have other ancestors
but these are the ones I like to remember

ancestor worship

people smelt bad in the old times
they had bad teeth, they were stupid
everything was ill fitting
so they fell about in sacks
their habits were appalling
no wonder they didn't live long

o they suffered much
but so much of it was self-inflicted
and they inflicted their world on us

of course they didn't know any better
they were so clumsy they broke
almost everything they touched
they were like clowns before the circus
was thought of

imagine them in bed
generation after generation
like your parents at it
but much worse
infinitely older uglier
o how ungainly
this getting a leg over
the dipping of the wilting wick

and that is why we worship them
because we're here
we're here!

An Attitude of Waiters

Eyes down, they won't see you.
Though it's only moments since
they pounced, so that you're seated
now. And now it is the season.
Let's have them stiff starched,
creased to bow, tuned to any tongue.
Their world is pigeon swift, yet
priestly, they will stand like herons,
have had the special training.
Collectively they know each
Other's signs. Once of the kingdom,
it is we seek their attention. This is
as arduous as prayer. Patience! Are
we virtuous? Sometimes we wave
the scripture at them. Kitchen will
have none of that. Even the specials
run out. Clock slogs. Appetite
makes monsters. It will pauperize
the soul. Cook knows how much
condiment. To pay's something like
Ragnarök. It matters little how
much silver you leave for them
on the plate. In heaven one imagines
them, crowded to whim, obsequious
of any peep. No greater delight in
their station but serve. Of course
you are already fed. Nor will the savour
ever lessen. Here on earth, we're all as
much for form. My model's Charlie
Chaplin, with his two great buffet trays
and absolutely no intention to pay.
Cigar for after, that's the style.
And let the world cough up.

English Weather

Umbrellas, raincoats, boots and gloves,
They are standard in this place,
In this so called Merry England,
The weather's a disgrace.

But the weather has a plus side,
It`s a little bit obscure,
But if you think about it,
The answer is quite sure.

The weather was so rotten,
Folks said 'it's not for me,'
And so they all jumped into ships,
And ventured out to sea.

They discovered tropic islands
Where the sun beams down and smiles,
'This is where we want to stay,
In tropical lands and isles.'

And that is how it came about,
The Empire came together,
And lasted out for centuries,
Due to lousy English weather!

Sesquipedalian

sesquipedalian: a foot and a half from sesoui and ped
*means long winded, using long words with many syllable*s.

How shall I put it?
To be a Sesquipedalian,
May appear to some
To be quite un-Australian.

When Australians speak English,
The words become short,
So the battle of language
Is the one to be fought.

When a simple mosquito,
Is reduced to a mozzie,
And in local language,
We call ourselves Ozzie.

And it's getting far worse,
I must really declare,
When 'yes' is too long,
And is shortened to 'yeh'.

We must do something drastic,
We must now take a punt,
Lest the whole English language
Is reduced to a grunt!

So, to deal with the problem,
I suggest that the cure,
Is to use really long words,
Of this I am sure.

We must now lift the language,
To a new lofty peg,
Like an 'ambulatory appendage',
Instead of a leg!

So let's lengthen our words,
This needs to be done,
And being a sesquipedalian,
Could turn out to be fun.

Yet this could all be a load
Of Taurofaecology,
A term that's connected
With bovine biology.

The Way the Light Fell

Out there in the desert,
The sun was shining bright,
The workers had to move the stones.
To try and clear the site

The place was out in Egypt,
Where they thought there was a tomb,
But they had to shift a lot of stone,
To make a little room.

They were working in a passage,
And they came up to a door,
The seal of clay was still intact,
As they were hoping for.

The rope that held the granite door,
Was still in good repair,
Although three thousand years had passed
Since living hands were there.

The seal was drawn and photographed,
Then it was taken down,
And there, between the granite doors,
A little crack was found.

The crack was then enlarged
With a chisel, and a brush,
But as the work was delicate,
It was not wise to rush.

And then a candle was inserted
To illuminate the depth,
And when Carter squinted through the hole
He could scarcely catch his breath.

Carter looked and muttered softly,
'I can't believe what I behold,
For where the light falls everywhere,
I see the glint of gold!'

It was November 1922,
When the candle broke the gloom,
And the light fell on the wealth and gold,
Of Tut-ank-amun's tomb!

Tea & A Bun

Here's to childhood, tea and a bun,
And splashing in puddles is always such fun,
With birthdays and parties, candles and cake,
No worries, no troubles, there's not much at stake.

But some aren't so lucky,
They get hunger and strife,
They don't taste a cake,
For the whole of their life,
Which is often cut short,
Through disease and neglect,
And are slaves to the adults
That's what I suspect.

So who is to blame?
They all pass the buck,
But if it's a banknote,
Into pockets they tuck,
Then send them to banks
With secret accounts,
And let them pile up
To gigantic amounts.

When they get to the Gate,
There's a question, 'How come,
You've amassed in your bank
Such a sizeable sum?'

He'll hear out their answer,
And then with a frown,
Put them all in the lift,
That's headed, straight down.

So much for them,
But what about us?
We'd better do something,
Or we might miss the bus.

Let us act as we should,
So that when we are done,
All children worldwide
Can have tea and a bun!

The Lion Tamer

It would have been alright,
If the lion wasn't cross,
'Cos it hadn't had its breakfast,
And it thought it was the boss.

But it would have been alright,
If when he got into the cage,
He hadn't trod upon the lion's tail,
And provoked a fearful rage.

But it would have been alright,
If he hadn't got all scared,
And tried to run out from the cage,
When the lion's temper flared.

But it would have been alright,
If he'd thought to close the door,
And the lion hadn't got outside,
And evened up the score!

Disquiet

staring down an empty alley
a lone figure, standing
enshrouded by a deathly pall
that hangs like rotten breath
from the drunk man's pores

I dare you to approach
he who has nothing to lose

Untitled

How far between heaven and hell.
The blink of an eye,
a lifetime.

Where do you sit in this diorama?

Are you lucky, settled in the upper echelons.
Glancing down, occasionally.
Sparing no thought, believing
nirvana is for the righteous.

Do you sit in the middle?
With more understanding
about the highs and lows of life.
Peering upwards, at times,
glancing down with trepidation.
Holding on.

Or are you on the long winding road,
the steep descent?
A narrow ledge,
no room for turning.
A one-way lane.

Like a stone, gathering momentum,
you hurl towards the gates of hell
with little chance of redemption.

Only radiant heat
from bottomless pits
rises to greet you.

Anorexia Nervosa

(you will see me)

aged
before time
thin
death, on show

private grief
a public display
you will see me, you cry
you will see me
I cannot be ignored

I see you
I see straight through you
your misery, despair
I will stare at you
like others stare at you

I watch this macabre dance
this slow disintegration
mind, body, soul
folding into yourself
simply disappearing

JULIE FREDERICKS

Father

a small smudge
rusted red, clay-like
clung to his nostril

lavender, distilled,
burns in the semi-darkness
death though, permeates

no solace to be found
in the blackness of that night
in his chair, in his house

JULIE FREDERICKS

Of you and me . . .

the face and body of my desire
to run a hand along your arm
or stroke your face
to hold your hand and feel the life
that emanates from a single touch

I look into your eyes
and feel I am lost
to let myself go
abandoned to the feeling
of lust, or love
at last a feeling coursing through my veins
makes me want to cry

better this image
than the harsh reality
of life, of problems, of dirty rubbish

I want to close my eyes
and dream of a perfect life
Of you and me . . .

Aliens

The latest chapter
In the Irish Book of Invasions
Stalking the hillsides
One-legged giants
Three arms in slow semaphore
To opposite horizons

The skeletal white army
Has landed
But they mean us no harm
The wind is their food
And light is their gift to us

Dreaming of the New Camden

Down the canals on paddle boards
The weekend hordes
Assemble
In flowing rags a guitarist solos from the hip
As the first to dare prepares
To plummet
From the electric slippery dip
Sparks flying from between his teeth

I've moved into an old boutique
Just off the high road
Which is kind of neat
But the door is only two feet high
Difficult with a greatcoat on
Never mind stilettos
The cobbled streets wind
Through jugglers and mimes and
T-shirts shouting manifestoes

I order an espresso
And find there what I'm looking for
Precisely
And try to find the price by
Searching for my glasses
I empty pockets
Of all classes of possessions
A procession of all I've ever owned
Till my whole life sits in front of me
Is this it? I think.
In its entirety
Is this it all?

And in the hall a girl slinks by
As I write poetry on my phone.
She winks
and asks if I'm a Gemini
I ask if she's alone.

Echoes

For Dee

A clatter from the kitchen
Footsteps in the stairs
Dusty on the stereo
Laughter in the air
The clickety click of Afghan paws
On painted floors
And from the back
The clackety clack of you
Slightly hungover
Knitting pullovers
For all of your lovers

Escape from Shanghai

Shanghai dinner high in the haze, a dizzy lazy
Suzan Szechuan cashew chicken sizzle
Hijacked into a Jenga stack skyscraper
KTV club drinking game, cocktail swizzle with
Dizzy business card shufflers booted suited sweaty fingers,
Leggy hostess with the Venus flytrap lashes lingers
With the karaoke singers.
Chinese, Cantonese, Japanese, Shanghainese,
None of these makes sense to me.
Who does what with whom and how much and what's expected,
And who are all these people supposed to be? I need to pee.
Toilet mirror walls and ceiling everything's reflected,
Contorted, distorted. Mission aborted.
Numbly stumbling, mumbling which way's out?
Where's the door? What have you done with the floor?
Outside. Street side. Taxi side lights. Taxi door
Slams. Running late.
Phone translations, palpitations, perspiration
Saturation. Airport. How much? How far away?
What the hell time is it anyway?
Eyes wide open, eyes scared shut, eyes mesmerised
With the size and shape and how
Tectonic plates take all the weight
Of this crazy place
And how the millions stand the pace
As they race to the sky
And so do I, flying
As the pin prick lights start to thin.
Headphones, gin, head spin.
White noise, black out.
Oblivion.

Summer of 81

A recollection of a
Chance meeting on a missed connection
A fleeting history
Rudely smeared on a map of Europe
Written in booze
And wine soaked kisses
We flung ourselves at one another
We were young, we had all summer

Our Parisian passions
Fashioned in Montmartre
Were just the start
Our siestes crapuleuses
And boozy matinees
Amuse bouche for those
Louche ways
And passionate haze of
Those crazy European days

On to Roma
Comatose and overdosed
On cellars of Valpolicella
Our long siestas
Our beers our lire
In the fountain
Our negritas
Our margaritas
Our peach granitas
Our dolce vita . . .

Sweet slippery nights in Athena
The retsina sweat
Of our misdemeanours
Your perfume on my fingers
Still—
Those details linger, always will
With all the emotional debris
Do you remember me
To that degree?

And in Berlin when you left
With him
My solitary gin soaked crawl
Your name scrawled across the Wall
Your face in every drinking hall
My falling tears
My souvenirs
Of you
And the chance I somehow blew
When I was young
And had you that summer
In eighty one

The Anniversary

The Men were never allowed in the house
She never let them in
Their place was in the fields
Or eating potatoes and buttermilk in the lean to
When hay was won
Or cows calved

Not when the planes flew over
Not when young men went to war
(And
Thankfully
Returned)

Nor when this country
went to war with itself

Not even when, too old to run the place
She took to her bed
And the Men took over
Well maybe then

And now, years on,
The house rebuilt
And now our home
With ducks in the pen
And dogs by the hearth
We celebrate
With grandchildren
Cousins and friends
Looking back on busy lives
She looks down from the chimney breast
Happy to have family in the house

City Love

You look into your true love's eye
To see what terms & conditions apply

Although your offer of love is rejected
Your statutory rights are not affected

The sweetest love's in anticipating
The customer knows a call is waiting

Your call, more lovely than that of the linnet
Is charged at fifty-eight pence per minute

Counting the cost of true love's obsession
Failure to meet payments can mean repossession

How many I-love-you departures before you learn
Past performance is no guarantee of future return.

The Bony

When I shared a bed
in nineteen fifty-two or three
with my bony father, I was led
to believe that we
were alone;

now I can own
that when his bony frame
closed in upon my back
and he whispered something, my name?
into my bony neck,

behind him
lay *his* bony father, and, behind,
his bony grandfather, his bony great-
grandfather . . . all that long-lined
boniness, lying in state,

their collective bony weight
pulling him down, but slow,
a little heavier each year
until he finally let go
and I fear

he's here
now with the same bony crew,
light as a feathery ton:
O they have a job to do
But not a word to my son.

Incident

'Liquorice-legs' was what we called
each well-heeled daughter of the Union
in belted Burberry of emerald green
'the highest colour in the Orange Lodge!'
Venus on stilts of black.

Our daily homeward march went past
their High School, with its netball courts
the jolly smack of hockey sticks;
our only game the leap to snatch
the trophy-scalp beret.

'What the hell were you thinking of?'
(sex, of course, though not by name)
It could have been a tipping point:
curfew, reprisal, pogrom . . . instead
we were forcibly re-routed.

Proverbs For The Computer Age

An Apple a day keeps the hacker away

Baud news travels fast

Better to light one Intel than to cursor the darkness

When the mat's away the mouse will play

Necessity is the motherboard of invention

Every blog has its day

Fight virus with virus

All that twitters is not scrolled

Let sleeping laptops lie

Beware of geeks bearing gifs.

The Male Line

Once, my father tried to rouse the fire
—my mother being gone to early Mass—
by pouring paraffin from an old jam-jar.
So focused on the task he seemed to miss
the presence of his young son in the arch
of his bent legs, a child too keenly drawn
to adult action, always on the search
for something new—well, he would soon learn
that when the heady vapour caught a spark
All Hell Broke Loose—My God, how I whinged!
But when in better light she would remark
that my fair eyebrows looked like they'd been singed,
I saved my breath to cool my porridge, and he
just winked to seal our first complicity.

The Mathematical Barman

The mathematical barman
lives in a world of his own;
he's calculating the average size
of the bubbles in each pint
or the different combinations of coins
in the right change from a fiver
or the time it takes a drop from the optic
to reach the slatted floor.
But the customers all love him,
and not just because he never
says: 'You've had one too many!'
He likes to put it this way:
'There's three types of barman,
them that can count and them that can't.'

Anna Kerdijk Nicholson

Menu

Bread / Piadina with extra virgin olive oil and balsamic
Marinated olives
Grilled eggplant
Roasted pumpkin and sage
Bruschetta with tomato, basil and bocconcini

❧

Risotto with zucchini, parmesan & herbs

❧

Fennel, orange, and olive salad with rocket
Roast potatoes with smoked paprika
Sautéed greens

❧

Beef and eggplant meatballs in tomato sauce

❧

Gelato
Vanilla bean pannacotta with strawberries

❧

I am on a journey here. I put away my watch,
with no metronomic time I am left with senses:
is this hunger and is it sufficient to warrant a meal?
Life reduces to sustainability—input and output.
—Anna Kerdijk Nicholson from 'The world is a handkerchief,
   today I spread it across my knees'

          low notes
          of a single flute
          threads through
          the autumn wind
          moonlight on his hands
          —Dawn Bruce from 'low notes'

Sometimes I long to swim far out to sea
And let the waves swell over me;
Feel the breasts of mermaids
Pressed against my skin
—Geoff Cartwright from 'Sometimes'

Pears

After Stanley Kunitz

Light slants across this threshold,
the mortar smells damp.
I came here last when the trees
were in bud at the valley foot.

For days now I have rolled pears
in newsprint, placing each one
in rows in boxes.

When the autumn crocus is bitten
by cold and I'm by the fire
I will cut through the seal—
that dry gold-flecked outside—
starting at the wizened stalk,
the juice will pool on the plate.
I will suck my fingers.

The boxes are in the garage roof
all except one, which I will send
to you.
You will prise off the lid
and smell the orchard
after all these years.

Nine perfect pears: each one
filled with how the garden was
this long, dry summer,
wrapped in old football games,
school concerts and petty crimes.

ANNA KERDIJK NICHOLSON

We used to swing our legs
sitting on this sill, nudging
each other's elbows for room.
The light is low now:
it lays a pattern on the wall.

How and why

That which can be found in the sun
laying saplings across a road

How water tastes cold as the cabin was
this morning before the sun blazed

How the rocks in this field
make you nearly a thief

That turning this corner, every time,
sighting Pigeon House

Wingecaribee's weed-green path
you at ease on your taut horse

suggests new meaning
even if not made

What does it matter, this catalogue
passing places time and again

noticing here in sudden shade
how a notched rail fits a post

lichen where once raw blond,
figs alight with late afternoon lorikeets,

old handbag of an electrocuted bat
how the airfield cities this high-plains grass,

on the freeway, a shock of ginger broken cat
roar of a footy crowd reflected off the rear block

ANNA KERDIJK NICHOLSON

Catalytic nows, colour, eye-harvest
bring more, and more intense, to

that old crucible, bring near the new—
taking within, paying of respect

The mind travels

A stream of brown trout in a shallow river, the mind travels so much faster than language, that laggard which if you try to get it by the scruff eludes, while the brain's already gone through Harold Pinter's *The Caretaker* and an image of the characters on stage, compared it to a Manchester production of *Godot* seen in the round and how the rails at one's feet bit into one's arches, the sparse leaves on the tree at the end (ah there is hope), the journey to *Caretaker* in York down the A59 driving in Mum's maroon mini, D shouting at the other drivers 'what the fuck, can't you drive, can't you see we need to be let in' and a couple of near head-ons, to sit there in the dark to be coruscated and all that in the time it took to write the words after 'laggard' and before 'eludes', how can we capture the trout which have moved darkly, playing three dimensional chess with their speckled glistening bodies, beauty unheralded, unsung.

The world is a handkerchief, today I spread it across my knees

To S J Brier, with love

I

     I navigate the days in this place with the light of the sun
and sometimes the stars, but my movements are not to-the-degree,
and once commenced, my track does not engage or lose
the Great Southern Land, neither am I under orders
nor have 94 in my care. I am static. Only figuratively
could I go where others have never been.

I am on a journey here. I put away my watch,
with no metronomic time I am left with senses:
is this hunger and is it sufficient to warrant a meal?
Life reduces to sustainability—input and output.
It was safe without the doors locked, and again;
until it becomes a forgotten concern.
                              Where once
one has gone before, starts pattern, layering;
and with it comes the chance of comparison:
before like that, now like this.

II

                           When you and I journey,
there are many layers; memories, old jokes, we raise them
as cushions on which to recline. I drive the road to Whitby,
over the moors, dark gritty heath and Fylingdales' early warning
for war when, passing coaching inns, in a nithering May wind,
we cast off, warp out and you tell about tearing wall paper, mania,
withdrawal, fear; I am amazed how little rage (but after all,
since your breakdown it has taken us six years). It could have been
you at Columbine with an Uzi on remote-control TV. Or,
once again, face-to-face with *thieving savages*, like Cook,
you might have taken a hostage, but this time no gun could
save you. Dismembered.

217

III

        We must either continue or go back: we go on,
we have to go on, whatever happens now we have come this far,
the distance closes behind us like a clap.
We are grateful for small things and take them to heart:
fish & chips twice in Whitby, *two breads, two teas*;
being breathless, laughing; sheep outside our tent,
the farmer's moor-blasted hands;
your song to the sheepdog who loved you
and how we drank till the stars swam;
the way bluebells grow in Yorkshire woods; and how again,
on Rosebery Topping, the world was a handkerchief below you,
and I watched you spread it across your knees.

ANNA KERDIJK NICHOLSON

Today the distance between the threads of the net

Let us imagine it is the width of a chink of light
falling near a wife's foot as she passes her husband's door;
the worn dip in a butcher's block on the Mile End Road;
the width of a carriage rut in the mud in York;
the fatness of folded secret orders from the Admiralty;
or perhaps as thin as a quill in an ink pot
on the St Lawrence River; but how shall it be measured
now, and how will we know when it is done?

Canto XXXIV

red dog kicks up dust
racing to muster cows

Grace

Perhaps you move unthinkingly like a dancer,
and, instead of moving for me, you forget,
go to a beat that is only yours:

as life is not fiction, it reaches no crisis
or apogee, I glimpse a sliver of light
in my eye corner and we are in our skins again;

your teeth, ears and beard, the line
defining your lips, panting, our pillows and legs
akimbo and, as usual, we resume in a new tone,

and each time is stitched to each other time by,
say, your hand at the back of my head, an infinitely
tender holding, supporting the neck like bathing:

these will be the moments which I know my mother
mourns my father for still – the unspoken, a gesture
unmanufactured. Seeing these moments makes one rindless:

they are the twist which, cherry-red and glowing,
embroiders me to you in the dark.

DAWN BRUCE

after the storm
a luminous sky
screech of cockatoos

oystercatcher's skull . . .
empty eye socket gathers
raindrops and stars

evening news . . .
the drip
of ripe peach juice
as I watch refugees on tv
lining up for bread

DAWN BRUCE

longing for you
as I gaze out the window . . .
the distance
to that far away moon
and your unreachable grave

low notes
of a single flute
threads through
the autumn wind
moonlight on his hands

reading
all the witch marks
above the fireplace
I wonder what our graffiti
will say about us

Clybucca

Three days short of Christmas
In December '89,
The sleeping driver failed to take a turn.

Thirty-five lives ended
When two buses then collided
On that day that I turned thirty-five.

The carnage so affecting,
That marriages have severed
And a suicide was always on the cards.

The ghosts of that day haunt me,
Though I have no real relation
Than some coincidental confluence of numbers.

Early goodbyes

The day my father died,
I was a thousand miles away,
Preparing for the birth
Of my third child.

I visited him the week before,
Blinded momentarily
By shivering tears,
He in my arms,
(A first)
As I watched his stumbling, new found blindness
And heard his quaint complaint
That hospital sandwiches
Were bloody awful.
The last I heard from him.

(My mother too,
Disappeared before her due,
Stymied by a heartless canker,
Kidnapped by a childish idiocy,
Struggling to attend to the end
Of a gold fish bowl,
My goodbyes said years before
She knew she'd gone.)

In that final week,
Embracing his men children
Was a new aspiration.
He must have twigged to mortality.
I was peeved,
Needing it forty years before.
But better late than never,
Or some such platitude.
Well, we indulge the dying
And there was much besides to honour.

My mourning done,
At the later funeral
'but the trappings and the suits of woe',
I gave a eulogy
And comforted the grieving
I had never met.

Three weeks' after
That last meeting with my father,
I visited his hospital bed,
Blinded momentarily
By shivering tears,
He in my arms,
(A first)
This new child,
And hoped that, as his father,
I might love him as well as mine had me,
And wondered fleetingly
What my omissions might be.

Once Were Filial

Captive of his Facebook muse,
Girl-envied, arse-length hair unkempt,
He rams his Rammstein into idling ears,
And ruminates.

Leftovers lately nuked,
Keep him permanently mute.

When I ask,
What is it that you long for?
A base guffaw
Dismisses his affairs as none of mine.

A Gallic shrug
Replaces grace.

We once loved Shakespeare,
He and I.
Lamenting Friar Lawrence
Brought us both to grief,
And as we happy two
Watched Branagh
Imitate the action of the tiger
And hurl himself
Once more unto the breach,
I knew that
I loved nothing in the world
So well as he.

Hormonotones
Now shut him up in seeming discontent,
Yet I,
Uncertain of my place,
Fret, and can say nothing.

But when, as day begins,
He plants his wet, sleep-tasting lips
Upon my once adored, now aguecheeky chops,
I rue the urge to urge him to the toothpaste
And giddy as a girl I grin.

'See ya, dad' is what I crave,
And, 'See ya, dad' is what I get.
It's not to be or not to be,
But it's a start.

A Sudden Thing

To the click and the clack
Of the clock at the back
Of her bed on the wall by the hall,
She waited, patiently
For a week
To be found, felled
By failing arteries and the grog,
Forehead fractured on the cold, white tiles
And bleeding a lake.

Three weeks and odd days earlier,
He, too, sat like that
On a cluttered couch
Demanding, as always,
Instant attention.
As always, denied.

We buried them both,
Bickering brother and squabbling sister
Side by side for eternity
Or fifty years when the lease runs out
And the rot stops.

She slouched, that last time I saw her,
Wine in hand,
Studying a stain on the venetian blind.

I left a night early, to escape the contagion
Of her pack-a-day habit
And her couldn't-give-a-fuck cuisine
For my cocoon
In Sydney suburbia,
Bound front and back
And side to side
By loving embraces
They had never known,
To mourn, in company, my lonely brother.

Within a month, ere yet the salt,
Someone once said,
Had left our flushing eyes,
I was back in Brisbane
Summing up a second time,
In a two-minute snatch,
What she had taken fifty years and
More to do.

It was so sudden, we said.
Damn them both to hell
For rudeness.

We wept, we wailed, we gnashed our teeth,
We downed an ale or two.
We mused on the charred remains
That schizoid phantoms and black dogs
Left of their fire-bellied lives.

My mourning work for him undone,
I hide in my haven, *Again*
Still ringing in my ears.
Superstitiously I fear the phone
And study a stain on the venetian blind.

Sometimes

Sometimes I long to swim far out to sea
And let the waves swell over me;
Feel the breasts of mermaids
Pressed against my skin
As they seduce me to the deep
And keep me there,
Where nightmares lurk.

Sometimes I long to crawl inside a mountain
And feel the earth bear down on me,
Crushing me into a fossil
To be a puzzle
Centuries and more away,
Like micro fish
Or picnickers in old Pompeii.

Sometimes I long to lie upon a pyre
And let the flames unravel me,
As they convert my bones to ash
And turn my flesh to smoke,
So I could look upon the world
From high above
And fathom what the fuss has been.

Will He Return From Afghanistan?

In the creeping frog song dark,
Midsummer nightmares
Roil her blood.

Innocents are slaughtered
To serve salvation,
Eyes are blinded
By fire branding fathers;
Cries of mother love
Minced into silence.

.

Serpents lurk in conjured shadows
Cast by malevolent moons
And breeding spiders enter her sex.

A wide yawning chasm
Sucks her into its drowning sludge.

She wakes with a start
In the midnight dark.
She listens to the cracking of her heart.

David Malouf

Menu

Handmade focaccia, rosemary, sea salt
Herb frittata
Marinated olives
Hommus
Rocket, herb salad with balsamic
Beetroot labna
Chargrilled vegetables

❧

50 Shades of Green salad, green goddess dressing
The Incinerator hand cut chips

❧

Rotolo of ricotta and spinach with a slow braised tomato sauce

❧

Orgy of summer berries with a mascarpone
and champagne mouse,
raspberry sorbet and meringue

❧

this is my father's land
tangerine sunsets overlay ashes
meandering cow-trails
through clover and thistles
—Marilyn Humbert from 'Returning Home'

I stare into a sky of an ever-reaching blue
deep as my prior notion about it, furred sepia
round the edges from traces of fires or the slow creep
of macular degeneration.
—John Carey from 'Blue'

Shy gifts that come to us from a world that may not
even know we're here. Windfalls, scantlings.

Breaking a bough like breathy flute-notes, a row
of puffed white almond-blossom, the word in hiding

among newsprint that has other news to tell.
—David Malouf from 'Shy Gifts'

Beside the River

from the bridge
in early morn'
pale streetlights haze my shadow
the last star blinks off

the river is still and clear-eyed
patient for caress of early breeze
a stolen moment between unlikely lovers

stingrays wing lazily
across the sandy bed
sifting food

shy movements of other dwellers
catch my eye; flathead, flounder,
a school of slippery minnows
skim the dimpled bottom
and nudge rusting pylons
studded with oysters
clusters of mussels

seagulls stretch
on their rocky isle
a pelican slides upstream
feathers gold in the first rays of sun

MARILYN HUMBERT

Returning Home

this is my father's land
tangerine sunsets overlay ashes
meandering cow-trails
through clover and thistles
muddy water in furrowed drains
carries life, follows fences
on hard-knuckled plains
of Central Victoria

a crow's caw is my father's song
stirring milkers from pasture
I ramble behind swollen udders
dodging steaming puddles
piles of hot manure
red-dog nipping heels
to the shed

roan, white, brindle
sway-backed dairy shorthorns
herded on concrete
of the round yard
chewing cud, waiting
their turn to gift milk
the touch of my father's hands

dust settles
rouging withered stalks
staining bare feet
mum in her pinny doling grey-water
on geraniums in salt-crusted earth
scattering foraging chooks
westward a scratch of cloud
thickens with hope

MARILYN HUMBERT

waves of squawking cockatoos
the shadows of evening
cross my father's land

Ricco

I watch him, thin arms swinging,
monkey-climb the highest backyard tree
peering through leaf-layers
steel-blue eyes lure and hook.

I'm a snared fish, struggling
to comprehend the maternal pull
reeled in, left dangling in the sun.
Our shadows back to back.

His angel voice fills dark hours;
grace notes sail among planets,
gathering momentum, chasing comets
slipstreaming rivers of staring stars.

Some days he's a drummer boy—
sticks brushing a slow waltz
sticks pounding pirouettes, scraping taut skin
outmanoeuvring my understanding.

And he screams
my head is crammed with bouncing noise;
ideas yelling for attention
refusing to be quiet.

Agitated,
he lashes out:
viper's tongue tasting the air
turbine legs flailing.

His high-pitch wail
slices layers from this mother's love
falling useless under the press
of autistic feet.

Sonny

At his side, I'm the steel girder
bridging the gap

in this place of glass
of no reflections

I'm the eavesdropper
a watcher of my boy's unspooling

the monsters under his bed
the ghouls in his closet

his rainbows
mullock heaps of rhinestones.

I sit beside him on a worn-wood chair
a spectator . . .

his ballet
of precise steps

squeezed
together thin-line lips

hand shrouded ears
shutting out whispers

clinks of hail on the tin roof
the moaning wind.

Sonny waits for night to rise
a giant with many eyes

peering into his mind
and the entry-code changes daily.

Mars

Red sands shift
gripped by solar winds;
a ruthless blade scraping
barren mountains, sterile plains.

No one hears ice chiming
deep beneath the tilting poles,
nor the boatman's solo song
as he steers the dry canal.

And almost heard
are footfalls bound in permafrost
tattered shadows
on the crumbling crater walls.

Pasted in *the book of days*
ghosts tangled by winter's splintered grass
with broken spears and rusting shields
where weeping seas once lapped.

No one hears the thrumming drums
or sees a mother's tears,
forgotten fragments, gently cradled
in constant circling clouds

of rising dust
and soundless screams
on this dead world of Mars.

Love-in

From the hide I watch the troupe parade
marching across wrinkled mudflats
to the great basin's shallows.

Their beaks, scimitars slicing the air
gaggles of waders, pink feathers fluffed
form-up in the tidal swamp

and I'm struck, this déjà vu,
the first spark, a knowing sigh.
If only you were here.

In unison onyx bills, serenade
heads swivel atop necks like elastic
stretched . . . twist and twang

strutting at the dance party
a rave, in the mosh-pit, centre stage
near the edge-wash.

I hear your laughter . . .
an avian love-in.
If only you were here.

Panguna

Leavings from a mine on Bougainville,
a pool of slurry with a rainbow tinge on top
transmogrified into Art Doco at the Gallery.
The face of the local woman sifting and stirring
has the depth and texture of a map of sorrow.
The mine was a pot of gold to offshore stakeholders
till it went belly up, the jobs jobs jobs they promised,
nothing but a dirty trickle of royalties, then a past
and future that had lost all meaning. Thousands
of dead in the name of budget repair to the opaque
personal accounts of kleptocrats and the pale
myth of the sturdy integrity of a nation-state.
We could learn from this but haven't and won't,
about land loyally tenanted but never owned.

From the Gonzo Film Archive

U.S. Military Intelligence in full evolution
from exploding cigars and toxic wetsuits
designed for Fidel to staring at goats

disarmingly till their horns drop off
or wrapping themselves in a full-body bubble
of invisibility by flexing the toned muscles

of the psyche, the way a three-year-old plays
hide-and-seek by standing in the middle
of a paddock with his eyes shut (hiding)

or open instead of counting to fifty (seeking).
The liaison officer from Noosa suggests that
none of this would work on brush turkeys

who just keep coming down the aisle of
the supermarket making for the popcorn.
There are background flashes of J. Edgar Hoover

in a tutu, Patton in his invisible bubble of
competence, Colin Powell covering his eyes
so George W. won't find him and ask him

to please explain. From slapstick to Zen and back
in a pulsating diorama. I feel like a fly on the wall,
the prototype with the tiny camera, shooting sparks.

Blue

I stare into a sky of an ever-reaching blue
deep as my prior notion about it, furred sepia
round the edges from traces of fires or the slow creep
of macular degeneration. The affective shading
is for each his own business, colour of Summers past
when time slowed to a hackney canter or a Provencal
ramble through heathland of mimosa and lavender.
This is the blue you set off into on the upswing
of your life, with no sense of destination or gravity,
the blue whose immensity shrinks your every mistake,
sets no limit to your travels or callow meditations:
on the need to unlearn to believe your eyes, the need
for time to sway to the rhythm of the senses, on the nature
of blue, on the nature of nature, on the blue of blue.

Dream Homes

In my dreams I have often tapped into
the false memory of homes I have never lived in
slapped together from a kit of architectural
and narrative clichés: a harbourside flatette
with no definable features but outside stairs
and a dresser filled with unsecured secrets;
a spacious open-plan apartment with an
indoor garden tended by unseen hands;
a two-storey terrace with upstairs rooms
which were never used, lounges and libraries
with not a bedroom in sight. And none
of these homes was a primary residence,
all bolt-holes to escape to, safe houses
to hide the residue of unnamed crimes,
places to bring an unsuitable lover to
or work on the draft of an explosive memoir.

A diet of crime and espionage fiction might
explain the building-blocks but not the impulse.
An analyst might look for an unhappy child
with a self that fitted badly which he needed
a weekend retreat away from. The social realist
might posit something sterner and more mundane:
A North Shore Sydney boy obsessed with
Real Estate options? Who would have thought?

Landscape

From forty feet I see what must be a rural scene
as shapes and colours flattened and trapped
in a small rectangle on the larger white rectangle
of a gallery wall. Up close, I see the stories,
the language of Time's dimension—a story of wind
and weather in the sedge-grass, the silent belling
of a stag from the hilltop telling a story
of the seasons of love. I see the time
of the painting's composition, the sketches
and revisions, the signature and the full-stop.
The tarnish and craquelure start a new narrative
of chemical change, of a passage through arms
loving or covetous, the occupation of other walls,
of attics and sea-chests. I have enough grasp
of Art History to see the painter's sensibility
trapped in the conventions of an Age.
The viewers also tip their thimblefuls of time
into the sea it floats on. The security guard in mid-shift
sees his time tracing a rhombus like the path
of a billiard-ball bouncing off all four cushes. The time
of my own watching is defined by the presence of a tour group
in the next room and threatening to catch up.

I make my way out through the frame of the Exit
and down the steps, controlled by Laws of Motion
and Gravity, on the surface of a ball that spins in Space.
I feel myself moving from frame to frame
in the fix of a camera-lens under the direction
of what I can only call a great Eye,
that at some notional and arbitrary fixed point,
turns me into a fragment torn from a pageant—
a man without a story, treading air.

Unravelling

My dream has a twilight clarity, focus
and definition with a dominant image:
a cockatoo of an incandescent white,
screaming with paradoxical softness,
rubs noses with a cat of the same colour
but more muted, taking its light from within,
not from the setting sun or the rising moon.
It must be the Garden of Eden or somewhere
close by, perhaps Merimbula. The tribes
have come back, still watchful but more
at ease. Ben Boyd has issued a gruff
apology to man and beast and grows
sweet potatoes and bean-shoots. I'm seven
years old again and my back doesn't hurt.

The new Loaf

Each day delivers it
new-risen like the sun
out of centuries
of homely experiment,
till it sits,
a knife beside it,
packed warm in its crust.

Each crumb
a point of enlightenment.
Some gruff old rustic
in us chuckles
with pride at the sour
-sweet of what we trade
of sunlight for starch.

No grace to be said.
No prayerful
nod in any direction.
Field and flesh
were made one for the other
gratis. When we break it
all's mended. Kind are kin.

Aubade.com

Trending this morning
on Twitter   the same old

the nothing's new under
the noisy   the nosey as

that holds
the mesh and mash of things

together   Small wars
in the glass

the loss   the lost   the itch
and ache   all tossed

in and turned over

The blind   the bland as
blend   In bridal

groundfrost a long shadow
an antic

caucus of magpies
their exchanges

beyond the goss
and gotcha of next and now

aspiring
to the insubstantial

sexting of pure
presence that is birdcall

Retrospect

A day at the end of winter. Two young men,
hooded against the silvery thin rain

that lights the forest boughs, are making towards
a town that at this distance never gets closer.

One of them, not me, as he turns, impatient
for the other to catch up, wears even now when I meet his
      face

in dreams, the look of one already gone, already gone
too far into the forest: as when, last night

in sleep, I looked behind me out of the queue for an old
      movie and you
were there, hood thrown back, your stack

of dirty-blond hair misted with sky-wrack, and when
my heart leapt to greet you, No, your glance

in the old conspiratorial way insisted,
Don't speak, don't recognise me. So I did not

turn again but followed down the track,
to where, all those years back, you turned

and waited; and we went on
together at the bare end of winter, breath from our mouths

still clouding the damp air, our footsteps loud
on the rainlit cobbled street, down into Sèvres.

Earth Hour

It is on our hands, it is in our mouths at every breath, how not
remember? Called back
to nights when we were wildlife, before kindling
or kine, we sit behind moonlit
glass in our McMansions, cool
millions at rehearsal
here for our rendezvous each with his own
earth hour.
                   We are feral
at heart, unhouseled creatures. Mind
is the maker, mad for light, for enlightenment, this late admission
of darkness the cost, and the silence
on our tongue as we count the hour down—the coin we bring,
long hoarded just for this—the extended cry of our first coming
to this ambulant, airy
Schatzkammer and midden, our green accommodation tomb.

Shy Gifts

Shy gifts that come to us from a world that may not
even know we're here. Windfalls, scantlings.

Breaking a bough like breathy flute-notes, a row
of puffed white almond-blossom, the word in hiding

among newsprint that has other news to tell.
In a packed aisle at the supermarket, I catch

the eye of a wordless one-year-old, whale-blue,
unblinking. It looks right through me, recognising

what? Wisely mistrustful but unwisely
impulsive as we are, we take these givings

as ours and meant for us—why else so leap
to receive them?—and go home lighter

of step to the table set, the bed turned down, the book
laid open under the desk-lamp, pages astream

with lights like angels' wings, arched for take-off.

Radiance

Not all come to it
but some do, and serenely.

No saying
what party they are of

or what totem
animal walks with them.

Tobias the street-smart
teen has his screwball dog.

For some it is stillness,
or within the orders

of humdrum
the nudge, not so gentle,

of circumstance. For some
the fall across their path

at noon of a shadow
where none shuld be,

for some their own
shadow seen as not.

For some a wound, some
a gift; and for some

the wound is the gift.
When they

too become one
of the Grateful Dead, it is

the silence they leave
in a bowl, in a book

that speaks and may join us;
its presence,

waist high at our side,
a commotion, a companionable

cloud with the shape and smell of
an unknown familiar, call it

an angel. At his nod,
the weather we move in

shifts, the wind changes.
Catching

the mutinous struck infant
in us on the off-chance

smiling.

Contributors

Richard James Allen is an Australian-born poet whose writing has appeared widely in journals, anthologies, and online over forty years. His latest book, *The short story of you and I*, is forthcoming from UWA Publishing. Previous books of poetry, fiction and performance texts include *Fixing the Broken Nightingale* (Flying Island Books), *The Kamikaze Mind* (Brandl & Schlesinger) and *Thursday's Fictions* (Five Islands Press), shortlisted for the Kenneth Slessor Prize for Poetry. Richard has a critically acclaimed career as a multi-award-winning writer, director, choreographer and performer for stage and screen. He won the Chancellor's Award for most outstanding PhD thesis at the University of Technology, Sydney. www.physicaltv.com.au

Helen Bersten, OAM has enjoyed being part of the North Shore Poetry Project for the past few years and is delighted to be able to read her poetry at the dinners. She writes sporadically in between looking after family and friends as well as doing doggy day care for her elderly friend, Louise. She fills in her spare time continuing to act as a sub-editor for the Australian Jewish Historical Society and a reader on Radio 2RPH, both voluntary positions which she has held for many years.

Erina Booker has written poetry for most of her life. She has a Major in Literature within her Bachelor of Arts degree, and a post-graduate degree in Counselling. She knows the value of words, and the pauses between them. She enjoys exploring different forms of poetry, and has been sought after to contribute Ekphrastic poetry to art, and craft, exhibitions in North America and Australia. A major work has been an Ekphrastic collaboration between an artist in New York and herself. Apart from published collections, Erina publishes in various journals, including *Blue Heron Review*, *Wisconsin*, *The Grapevine*, Ithaca, NY, and *Eucalypt*, Sydney. Though having had other careers, she knows that poetry has always been her purpose.

Dawn Bruce is a widely published poet and creative writing tutor. She was coordinator of the awarding winning group Somerset Poets and leader of Harbourside Poets. She is presently the leader of Ozku (haiku) and Moonrise (tanka), both small master classes in Sydney. Her poetry collections, *Stinging the Silence*, *Tangible Shadows* and *Sketching Light* were published by Ginninderra Press. She is not sure if free verse gave her up or she gave up free verse . . . she only writes haiku, tanka and haibun now . . . but with a passion.

John Carey is an ex-teacher of French and Latin and a former actor. He has been published in *Contemporary Australian Poetry* (Puncher & Wattmann), *Best Australian Poems* and *Best Australian Poetry* plus the usual magazine suspects. The latest of his five collections is *Duck Soup & Swansongs* (Ginninderra Press 2018). John is known for comic and satirical poems but his quieter and more meditative pieces are just as important.

Geoff Cartwright is a former actor, now teacher and theatre director, occasional poet and passionate lover of riding-his-motorcycle-a-long-way. His love of the theatre, particularly Shakespeare has seen him perform and direct several outdoor productions for which he also has a passion. As the inaugural director of The Rough Hewn Theatre Troupe, which has been running since 2007, he has directed plays by Shakespeare, Racine, Dario Fo, Ray Mathew, Timberlake Wertenbaker, Moliere, Dylan Thomas, Anthony Burgess and Alana Valentine. Having ridden a motorcycle around twenty-two states of the USA in 2014 and around Australia in late 2017, he is ready to do it all again.

Eileen Chong is a Sydney poet who was born in Singapore. She is the author of six books, the most recent being *Rainforest* (2018), from Pitt Street Poetry. Her books have been highly commended for the Anne Elder Award, shortlisted for the Victorian Premier's Literary Award, and twice for the Prime Minister's Literary Award. www.eileenchong.com.au

Tricia Dearborn's poetry has been widely published in Australian literary journals, as well as in the UK, the US, Ireland and New Zealand. Her work is represented in anthologies including *Contemporary Australian Poetry* (2016), *Australian Poetry since 1788* (2011) and *The Best Australian*

Poems (2012 and 2010). She is on the editorial board of *Plumwood Mountain: An Australian Journal of Ecopoetry and Ecopoetics*. Her latest collection is *The Ringing World* (Puncher & Wattmann, 2012). Her next collection, *Autobiochemistry,* was completed with the support of an Australia Council grant and is forthcoming from UWA Publishing.

Benjamin Dodds is a Sydney-based poet who was born in the NSW Riverina. His debut collection *Regulator* was published by Puncher & Wattmann Poetry in 2014. His poetry and reviews have appeared in *Best Australian Poems, Stars Like Sand: Australian Speculative Poetry, Meanjin, Southerly, Cordite* and on ABC Radio National's *Poetica* program. A teacher and former laboratory technician, Dodds's current project explores the ethical and personal boundaries of scientific research through poetry.

Julie Fredericks was born in Sydney and has been living on the north shore for the past twenty years. Painting and poetry provide a source of meditation which takes her to a certain creative space, where there are no intrusions from a busy and at times chaotic mind. Her work is intuitive and inspired by life's experiences and observations. Julie is a very happy 'apprentice' of the North Shore Poetry Group.

After University **Col Grant** pursued a career in health services, as an academic in Australia and Hong Kong with numerous national and international publications. Later he followed up interests in social security at Brunel University. For several decades he has been writing poetry and is a regular contributor at functions of the North Shore Poetry Project and elsewhere. His poetry has been published in various formats including anthology, book, broadsheet and journal. He has a second book of poetry in preparation.

Alison Gorman grew up in Melbourne but has lived in Sydney for the past 20 years. After university, she worked as a speech pathologist in a brain injury rehabilitation team. Currently, she teaches creative writing to children at the Ku-ring-gai Arts Centre. Alison completed a Masters of Creative Writing at the University of Sydney in 2014 where she met Philip Porter. She has been reading as a local poet at Rubino's since 2013.

Her poems have been published in Australian literary journals and two anthologies. She won the Dorothy Porter prize for poetry in 2016.

Kevin Hart's most recent books of poems are *Wild Track: New and Selected Poems* (Notre Dame UP, 2015) and *Barefoot* (Notre Dame UP, 2018). He teaches at the University of Virginia. He is currently writing a new book of poems, *Firefly*.

After two amazing decades in the dynamic landscape of the Exhibition and Events industry, **Sarnie Hay** now works as a Fashion Consultant for one of Australia's well-known and iconic brands. Her spare time is taken up with writing poetry, or working in the Gunyah Community Garden that she created three years ago. It is not only nature that inspires her poetry, but a passion for preserving Sydney's unique and charming architecture. She's lucky to live near the harbour, where she often pauses in a Secret Garden to admire the beautiful cityscape of Sydney.

Rosemary Huisman is Honorary Associate Professor in English at The University of Sydney. Her academic publications include *The Written Poem, Semiotic Conventions from Old to Modern English* (1998; 2000). Her own volume of poetry, *The Possibility of Winds*, was published in 2005. In 2017, her poem, 'it is as if', was 'highly commended' in the Bruce Dawe Poetry Prize.

Marilyn Humbert lives in the Northern suburbs of Sydney. Her tanka and haiku appear in international and Australian journals, anthologies and online. Some of her free verse poems have been awarded prizes in competitions and some have been published.

Christopher (Kit) Kelen has a dozen full length collections in English as well as translated books of poetry in Chinese, Portuguese, French, Italian, Spanish, Indonesian, Swedish and Filipino. His next volume of poetry is *Poor Man's Coat—Hardanger Poems*, to be published by UWAP in 2018. In 2017, Kit was shortlisted twice for the Montreal Poetry Prize and won the Local Award in the Newcastle Poetry Prize. Emeritus Professor at the University of Macau, where he taught for many years, in 2017, Kit

Kelen was awarded an honorary doctorate by the University of Malmö, in Sweden.

Anna Kerdijk Nicholson's four collections of poetry are *The Bundanon Cantos* (2003), *What was Lost* (2007), *Possession* (2010) and *Everyday Epic* (2015). In 2010, *Possession* won the Victorian Premier's Prize and the Wesley Michel Wright Prize and in 2011 was shortlisted for the ACT and the NSW Premiers' Prizes. A song cycle and orchestral pieces written on Anna's poetry are in performance in Europe. For many years she served on the boards of the Poets Union and its national successor, Australian Poetry and she co-edited the literary journal, *Five Bells*. Born in Yorkshire, she now lives in rural NSW.

Andy Kissane lives in Bardwell Park and writes poetry and fiction. He has published a novel, a book of short stories, *The Swarm,* and four books of poetry. Recent poetry collections include *Out to Lunch* and *Radiance* (Puncher & Wattmann, 2014), which was shortlisted for the 2015 Victorian Premier's Prize for Poetry, the 2016 Adelaide Festival Awards for Literature, and the 2016 Western Australian Premier's Awards for Poetry. He was the winner of the 2017 Tom Collins Poetry Prize. He has read his work in Ireland, England, Austria and many venues in Australia. http://andykissane.com

David Malouf is the author of nine collections of poetry since *Bicycle and other Poems* (UQP, 1970), the latest *Typewriter Music* (UQP, 2007) and *Earth Hour* (UQP, 2014). A new collection, *An Open Book*, will be published in October, 2018.

Stephen Mason, Melbourne, born in 1955 and has enjoyed reading local and translated traditional and contemporary poetry since he was about 15. He started writing his own attempts at poetry in the early seventies. His favourite poets back then were Judith Wright and A.D. Hope, Elizabeth Bishop and Robert Lowell. His contemporary favourite Australian poets are Kevin Hart and Clair Potter, MTC. Cronin and Peter Boyle. His own work was first published in *Meanjin* 3/84. Recently he had a self-published novella-poem shortlisted in the Woollahra Writers'

Word Festival: Irina Dunn interviewed him, and recommended his book, *Silk Music*, as a good read.

Pam Morris grew up enjoying the beach at Bondi in the era of trams. The passage of time and the expanse of distance are in her thoughts. Pam is a member of the Youngstreet Poets and her work has been published in Youngstreet Anthologies. A collection of her poems, *In the Breathing Space,* was published in 2013. She enjoys contributing to the Café Poets and NS Poetry Project readings, and six of Pam's poems were included in the Café Poets Anthology, *A Patch of Sun,* in 2016.

Gary McCartney is a designer, artist and writer originally from Northern Ireland. His company, McCartney Design, has won several Australian and international design awards. His poetry has been published in the first Café Poets' Anthology, *A Patch of Sun,* and his short stories have appeared in *Overland, Aurealis* and *The Wine Dark Sea.* Gary's work is influenced by a sense of place and the strange idiosyncrasies of humankind.

Iggy McGovern lives in Dublin, where he is Fellow Emeritus in Physics at Trinity College. He has published three collections of poetry with Dedalus Press, *The King of Suburbia,* (2005), *Safe House* (2010) and *The Eyes of Isaac Newton* (2017). *A Mystic Dream of Four*, a poetic biography of the 19th century mathematician William Rowan Hamilton, was published by Quaternia Press in 2013. Awards include the Hennessy Literary Award for Poetry and the Glen Dimplex New Writers Award for Poetry.

Mickey Millner arrived on the planet on the 28th May 1932. He grew up in Johannesburg where he studied Pharmacy. In 1963 he married 'the girl with the gentian eyes'. They have three sons, and five grandchildren. While this was going on, he started writing humorous poetry, and putting Bible stories into verse. In 1978, the family emigrated to Sydney. Mickey has recently had poems published in the North Shore Poetry Project's Anthology, *A Patch of Sun* and is about to launch his own collection of poems.

Charles Murray, born Dublin, Ireland 1940, migrated to Australia in 1963, with the intention of working in the teaching profession, however, fate and circumstance led him to a career in the heavy engineering and construction industries in which he is still involved as a consultant to the Civil, Marine and Defence industries in the design and commissioning of specialist lifting technology. He has been dedicated to creative writing since his student days and as a proactive peace-loving social justice activist, his poetry and memoir pieces have been published in the broadsheet, tabloid and magazine media throughout Australia and overseas.

Philip Porter started writing poetry about a dozen years ago and has been published in a variety of magazines and journals in a number of countries. His main enthusiasm over the past 6 years has been convening the North Shore Poetry Project which offers regular Poetry Workshops and reading spaces for local and established poets.

Somewhere in **Frances Roberts's** childhood, poetry became her response to feelings aroused by the world around her. The bushland in which she lived was her first focus and, a few years after that, she became fascinated by the role of language in human interactions. A career in psychology brought the two worlds together. She won a Haiku competition, which boosted her confidence and led to her submitting 6 poems to *Eureka Street* who published them.

Robyn Rowland is an Irish-Australian citizen living in both countries. She regularly works in Turkey. She has written 13 books, 10 of poetry. Her latest books are *Mosaics from the Map* (Doire Press, Galway, 2018) and her bi-lingual *This Intimate War Gallipoli/*Çanakkale *1915 – İçli Dışlı Bir Savaş: Gelibolu/*Çanakkale *1915* (republished, Spinifex Press, Australia, 2018). Turkish trans. Mehmet Ali Çelikel. Robyn's poetry appears in national and international journals and in over forty anthologies, including eight editions of *Best Australian Poems*. Her work is on film at the National Irish Poetry Archives, James Joyce Library, UCD. Dublin.

Alex Skovron is the author of six poetry collections, a prose novella and a book of short stories, *The Man who Took to his Bed* (2017). His latest volume of poetry, *Towards the Equator: New & Selected Poems* (2014), was shortlisted in the Prime Minister's Literary Awards. Alex's numerous public readings include appearances in China, Serbia, India, Ireland, Macedonia, and on Norfolk Island. His poetry has been translated into French, Chinese, Polish, Spanish and Dutch, and his novella *The Poet* is available in Czech. He lives in Melbourne.

Thomas Thorpe is a graduate of Nottingham and Sydney Universities, and an Associate of the National Trust (NSW). Commissioned in the RAF, he spent 2½ years in the Libyan desert learning the value of water and respect for the sun. Recruited by NSW Department of Education he sailed to Australia in 1962—a *ten quid pom*. He worked as a teacher, and then in teacher education, heading a department of Australian Catholic University. A director of the former NSW Poets' Union Inc., he produced poetry events for Sydney WEA, and for Kirribilli Neighbourhood Centre. He established and coordinates *Poetry at the Sydney Mechanics' School of Arts*. He has published in Australia, New Zealand, Romania, and the UK.

John Upton was a professional playwright and had written for more than 20 Australian television series as well as having five stage plays produced. His political comedy *MACHIAVELLI, MACHIAVELLI* won the Australian Writers Guild award for Best New Play. His poetry collection, *Embracing the Razor*, was published by Puncher & Wattmann in 2014 and his poetry has been widely published in magazines and journals including *The Sydney Morning Herald, The Canberra Times, Cordite, Quadrant* and many other magazines and anthologies.

Acknowledgements

Erina Booker
'Quaternary: I Dust to Dust', 'IV Igneous', 'VII Fissure', 'Icon', 'Ariadne's Lament': *A Cobbled Path*
'The Turning of the Leaves': *Coalescence*

Dawn Bruce
'after the storm': *Presence*
'oystercatcher's skull': *Windfall*
'evening news': *Ribbons*
'longing for you': *Red Lights*
'low notes': *Eucalypt*
'reading': *Skylark*

John Carey
'Blue' : *Contemporary Australian Poetry*
'Dream Homes': *Irises* (Canberra VC Prize Long List 2017)

Eileen Chong
'Burning Rice', 'Lu Xun, your hands': *Burning Rice*
'Only A Peony': *Peony*
'Magnolia', 'Painting Red Orchids', 'Seven in the Bamboo': *Painting Red Orchids*

Tricia Dearborn
'The changes', 'Come in, lie down', Memo': *The Ringing World*
'Hydrogen': *Canberra Times*
'Calcium': *Cordite Poetry Review*
'Perimenopause as rocket science': *Verity La*

Benjamin Dodds
'Regulator': *Etchings*
'Thinning our little herd': *Blue Dog*
'The spiders are here': *Writreview*

ACKNOWLEDGEMENTS

'Prodigal son (and his partner)': *Australian Poetry Members' Anthology 2012*
'Space age': *Mascara Literary Review*
'Surrogacy': *Cordite Poetry Review*

Kevin Hart
'Invective': *The Australian*
'Rain', 'New Uz': *Southerly*
'Gillyflower', 'The Rat Summons', 'Spring Wheat': *Arena*

Marilyn Humbert
'Ricco', 'Mars': *Award Winning Australian Writing*
'Sonny': *Ear to Earth Henry Kendall Anthology*

Kit Kelen
'let everything go wild today', 'practical hypothetical', 'Blokes', 'Magyar idyll', 'ancestor worship', 'An Attitude of Waiters': *a pocket kit 2*

Anna Kerdijk Nicholson
'Pears', 'How and Why', 'The mind': *Everyday Epic*
'The world is a handkerchief, today I spread it across my knees', 'Today the distance between the threads of the net': *Possession: Poems about the voyage of Lt James Cook in the Endeavour 1768-1771*
'Canto XXXIV: Grace': *The Bundanon Cantos*

Andy Kissane
'Loaves and Days', 'The Carpet Weaver': *Out to Lunch*
'The Street Vendor's Lament', 'It Begins with Darkness': *Radiance*
'3am': *Every Night They Dance*
'The Book of Screams': *Cordite Poetry Review*

David Malouf
'Retrospect', 'Earth Hour', 'Shy Gifts', 'Radiance': *Earth Hour*
'Aubade.com', 'The New Loaf': *An Open Book*

ACKNOWLEDGEMENTS

Iggy McGovern
'City Love, The Bony': *The King of Suburbia*
'Incident', 'Proverbs For The Computer Age': *Safe House*
'The Male Line', 'The Mathematical Barman': *The Eyes of Isaac Newton*

Charles Murray
'The Fields of Grief': *Royal Australian Army Medical Corps Magazine*

Philip Porter
'urban affection': The quote, *'my arm ever so lightly'* is from Walt
Whitman. The quote 'a mouthful of air' is from W.B. Yeats.
'The Blue Lady Lamp': The quote, *'So much depends/upon'* is from 'The
Red Wheelbarrow' by William Carlos Williams.
Tanka: *Eucalypt*

Robyn Rowland
'Stone Child', 'Sliver of Australian Summer': *Mosaics from the Map*
'Hero Unmasked', 'Known by heart': *Line of Drift*
'The Dead', 'When he was Young, Once': *This Intimate War Gallipoli/
Çanakkale 1915 – İçli Dışlı Bir Savaş: Gelibolu/Çanakkale 1915*

Alex Skovron
'Visitation': *Australian Poetry Journal*
'Legend': *Towards the Equator: New & Selected Poems*
'Serenade': *Meanjin*

Thomas Thorpe
'Legacy in Chatswood Mall': *Studio*
'Locomotion': *The Mozzie*
'Sometimes at Dawn': *Versuri albe pentru zile negre,*

John Upton
'Hidden', 'Angel': *The Weekend Australian*
'Crossing Galanta': *Overland*

Editor's Note

Thanks again to Australian Poetry who created the Café Poets Project several years ago which led to the publication of our first Anthology, *A Patch of Sun*, and now this, our second, *The Intimacy of Strangers*. Also, to our constant sponsors; Intermain Pty Ltd, Dawn Bruce, Marry Me Gwen, Philip Porter Consulting and the restaurants, Rubinos and The Incinerator. Special thanks to John Carey, who is both a local and guest poet, for his advice and aid in sourcing excellent guest poets as well as Julie Fredericks for her assistance in typing several aspects of the manuscript. Many thanks also to Kath Norris who designed all the Poetry Night flyers and posters. At the heart of this project are the many local poets who attend our weekly Monday morning workshop and our monthly Tuesday night readings without whose generosity of spirit, talent and general enthusiasm for poetry and each other none of this would have been possible. Finally, I want to thank my co-editor and friend, Andy Kissane, who has been unstinting in his contribution to the creation of *The Intimacy of Strangers*. Without his forensic eye, poetic knowledge and patience this edition would not have made it into your hands.

—Philip Porter